OUT OF
THE TRAP

OUT OF
THE TRAP

*Selected Lectures
of Alan W. Watts*

Edited by
Mark Watts

South Bend, Indiana

OUT OF THE TRAP

and books
702 South Michigan, South Bend, Indiana 46618

Library of Congress Catalog Number: 85-0084565

International Standard Book Number: 0-89708-147-1

3 4 5 6 7 8 9

Printed in the United States of America

Cover illustration: The banyon tree is one of the wonders of Indian vegetation; it is continually increasing—every branch proceeding from the trunk, throws out long fibres, which descend and take root in the earth.

Additional copies available:
the distributors
702 South Michigan
South Bend, IN 46618

Dedicated to Henry 'Sandy' Jacobs

Available from:

the distributors
702 S. Michigan
South Bend, IN 46618

CONTENTS

PREFACE

The following lectures have been selected from the Alan Watts tape library, a collection of many hours of recordings made by Alan Watts during the sixties and early seventies. As the title Out Of The Trap implies, these selections are excellent examples of Watts's uncanny ability to point to ideas which limit our horizons and keep us perpetually bound with the ego-self. Alan Watts saw through the game and was prone to laugh at the great hoax that we create for ourselves through ignorance of our true nature. And our true nature is not a 'higher self' to be discovered, but rather the true divinity of daily life as found—"in all the details."

In this collection we find a more accurate description of nature—not as something separate from man, but in its original sense, as the virtues or characteristics of nature, including the seemingly senseless expressions of mankind run amuck with aimless technology and its resulting inevitable alienation.

Drawing from the philosophies of the Eastern and Western world Watts brings us a uniquely balanced way of finding out who we really are. Although it may be strange to

CONTENTS

say that a timeless philosophy has come of age, I could not help but think while preparing this manuscript that my father's words will find a more receptive audience today than in the sixties when he was considered by some to be rather 'far out!' Historical events and scientific advances of the seventies have brought us to the realization that indeed man is capable of anything, and now perhaps we are possibly better prepared to listen to his warm and personal syntheses of the most important aspects of religious philosophy and human psychology.

In perparing this text, great effort has been made to preserve the flavor and content of his original talks. For this reason you may find the following chapters to differ from his written style, but by reading aloud, you may recapture his play of words and wisdom.

Mark Watts

Comments welcome

Post Office Box 938
Point Reyes Station
California - 94956

1

MAN'S PLACE
IN NATURE

I was talking to you this morning about the basic philosophy of nature that underlies Far Eastern culture, and explaining why it's so important for us in the West to understand this, so that we can encourage the Japanese people to re-understand it—because they are in danger of following some of our wildest excesses, and doing things that will destroy our environment. You see, a great deal of what we have done by way of technological development is based on the idea that man is at war with nature, and that in turn is based on the idea, which is a really a 19th century myth, that intelligence, values, love, humane feelings, etc. exist only within the borders of the human skin. And that outside those borders the world is nothing but a howling waste of blind energy, rampant libido, and total stupidity.

This you see, is the extreme accentuation of the platonic Christian feeling as man as not belonging in this world, of being a spirit imprisoned in matter. And it's reflected in our popular phraseology. "I came into this world." "I face facts." "I encounter reality." It's something that goes "boom" right against you like that!

But all this is contrary to the facts. We didn't come into this world—we grew out of it, in the same way that apples grow out of an apple tree. And if apples are symptomatic of an apple tree, I'm sure that after all, this tree apples—when you find a world upon which human beings are growing, then this world is humane, because it humans.

Only we seek to deny our Mother, and to renounce our origins, as if somehow we were lonely specimens in this world, who don't really belong here, and who are aliens in an environment of consisting mostly of rock and fire, and mechanical electronic phenomena, which has no interest in us whatsoever, except maybe a little bit in us as a whole, as a species. You've heard all these phrases, "Nature cares nothing for the individual, but only for the species." "Nature as in tooth and claw." "Nature is dog-eat-dog," or as the Hindus call it *Matsyanaya* the Law of the Sharks. And so; also a very popular idea of the 19th century running over into the common sense of the 20th, is that we belong as human beings on some very small, unimportant spec of dust, on the outer fringes of a very small galaxy, in the middle of millions and millions of much more important galaxies. And all this thinking is pure mythology.

Let me go in a little bit to the history of it, because it's important for us as Westerners to know something about the history of the evolution of our own ideas that brought this state of mind about. We grew up as a culture in a very different idea, where the universe was seen as something in which the earth was at the center, and everything was arranged around us, in a way that we of course as living organisms naturally see the world. We see it from the center, and everything surrounds us. And so, this geocentric picture of the world was however, one in which every human being was fantastically important, because *you* were a child of God, and you were watched day in, day out, by your loving and judging father in Heaven. And you, because you have an eternal life, are infinitely important in the eyes of this God.

I have a friend who's a convert to Roman Catholicism, and is a very sophisticated and witty woman. And in her bathroom she had one of those old-fashioned toilets with a pull-tank on the top, and a pipe down to the toilet seat. And fastened on this pipe there was a little plaque which had on it nothing but an eye. And underneath was written in Old English Gothic style letters: "Thou God sees me." So everywhere is that watching eye, that examines you, and at the same time as it knows you, it causes your existence. By knowing you, God creates you, because you are an act of His creative imagination. And so you are desperately important.

But Western people got this feeling that this became too embarrassing. You know how it was as a child, when you were working in school, and the teacher walked around behind your back, and looked over while you were working, and you always felt put off. While the teacher is watching you, you are non-plussed. You want to *finish* the work and *then* show it to the teacher. There is a problem. Never show anything unfinished to children or to fools. And children feel this very strongly about their teachers. They want to finish it before it's looked at.

So in exactly the same way, it's embarrassing to feel that your inmost thoughts and your every decision is constantly being watched by a critic, however beneficent and however loving that critic may be, that you are always under judgement. To put this to a person is to bug him totally. Indeed, it's one of the techniques used in Zen for putting people into a very strange state of mind. You are always under watch.

It was a great relief for the Western world when we could decide that there was no-one watching us. Better a universe that is completely stupid than one that is too intelligent. And so, it was necessary for our peace of mind, and for our relief that during the 19th century particularly, we got rid of God, and found then that the universe surrounding us was supremely unintelligent, and was indeed a universe in which we, as intelligent beings, were nothing more than an accident. But then, having discovered this to be so, we had to take every conceivable step, and muster all possible energy to make this accident continue, and to make it dominate the show. The price that we paid for getting rid of God was rather terrible. It was the price of feeling ourselves to be natural flukes, in the middle of cosmos quite other than ourselves—cold, alien, and utterly stupid, going along rather mechanically, on rather rigid laws, but heartless.

This attitude provoked in Western man a fury to beat nature into submission. And so, we talk about war *against* nature. When we climb a mountain like Everest, we have *conquered* Everest. When we get out enormous phallic rockets and boom them out into space, we're conquering space. And all the symbols we use for our conquest of nature are hostile: rockets, bulldozers... this whole attitude of dominating *it*, and mastering *it*.

Whereas a Chinese person might say, when you climb a high mountain, "You conquer it? Why this unfriendly feeling? Aren't you glad the mountain could lift you up so high in the air, so as to enjoy the view?" So this technology that we have developed, in the hands of people who feel hostile to nature is very dangerous. But the same technology in the hands of people who felt that they belong in this universe could be enormously creative. I'm not talking some kind of primitivism, as if we should really get rid of all technology, and go back to being a kind of primitive people, but rather that, in the hands of people who really know that they belong in this world, and are not strangers in it, technology could be a wonderful thing. For one sees, in the art forms that have been developed through this philosophy, that we have a combination. My friend Sabro Hasegawa, a great Japanese artist of modern times, used to call it the "controlled accident." That there is on one hand, the unexpected thing that happens of itself that nobody could predict—that's the accident. And there is, on the other hand, prediction, control, the possibility of directing something along certain lines, just as when the sailor moves against the wind, with the power of the wind, he is using skill to control the wind. So, in the same way our controlling things has a place, but it is with the accidental world of nature, rather than against it.

So then, this is why the philosophy of nature, and the civilization of the Far East is immensely important to us to understand, with our vast technical powers. And again in turn we, understanding that point of view, are immensely important to the people of the Far East, so as to help them not to be too intoxicated by our way of doing things. There's a long, long story about why technology developed in the West first, rather than in the Far East, and I'm not going to go into that for the moment. But the important thing about this whole philosophy of nature, and of man's place in nature is that this Taoist, and later Zen Buddhist, and Shinto feeling about man's place in the world is today corroborated by the most advanced thinking in the biological and physical sciences. Now, I can't stress that too much.

Science is primarily description, accurate description of what's happening, with the idea that if you describe what is happening accurately, you're way of describing things will become a way of measuring things. And that this in turn will enable you to predict what is going to happen. And this will build you some measure of control over the world. The people who are most expert in describing, and who are most expert in predicting are the first people to recognize the limitations of what they're doing.

First of all, consider what one has to do in science, in a very simple experiment, in which you want to study a fluid in a test tube, and describe what is in that fluid so accurately, that you must isolate that fluid from what are called "unmeasurable variables". I have a fluid in a test tube, and I want to describe it accurately, but every time the temperature changes, my fluid changes, so I want to keep it free from changes of temperature. This already implies an air conditioning system. Also, I don't want my fluid to be jiggled, because that may alter it. So I've got to protect it from trucks that go by the lab. And so I have to build a special bump-proof room, where trucks won't jiggle it. Also, I have to be very careful that when I look at this fluid I won't breathe on it, and affect it in that way. And that the temperature of my body, as I approach it won't alter it. And I suddenly discover that this fluid in a test tube is the most difficult thing to isolate in all the world. Because everything I do about it affects it. I cannot take that fluid in a test tube and take it out of the rest of the universe, and make it separate and all by itself.

A scientist is the first to notice this. Furthermore, he knows not only that it's his bodily approach that alters things, he finally discovers, in studying quantum theory, that looking at things changes them. So when we study the behavior of electrons, and all those sub-atomic particles, we find out that the means we use to observe them changes them. What we really want to know is, what are they doing when we're not looking at them? Does the light in the refrigerator really go out when you close the door? So what will it do when it's not being watched? Because we found out that watching them affects them. Why, because of course, in order to observe the behavior of sub-nuclear particles, we have to shine lights on them, as it were. We have to bombard them with other nuclear particles, and this changes them. And so we get to the point where we can know the velocity of the particle, without knowing its position, or know its position without knowing its velocity. You can't know both at the same time. What all that is telling us is—we cannot stand aside as an independent observer of this world, because you the observer are what you're observing. You're inseparable from it.

Let me put it in another way. Science, I said, was accurate description. We want to describe the behavior of any given organism, whether it's human, or whether it's an ant, or whatever it is. Now how will you tell, how will you say what an ant is doing without describing at the same time, the field or the environment in which the ant is doing it. You can't say that an ant is walking, if all you can describe is that this ant is just wiggling its legs. You have to describe the ground over which the ant is walking, to describe walking. You have to set up directions, points of the compass, etc. And so, soon you have to describe all the ant's friends and relations. You have to describe its food sources. And so you soon discover that although you thought you were talking about an ant, what you are actually talking about is an ant environment... a total situation from which the ant is inseparable. You're describing the behavior of the environment in which ants are found, and that includes the behavior of ants.

So too, human behavior involves first of all, the description of the social context in which human beings do things. You can't describe the behavior of an individual, except in the context of a society. You'll have to describe his language. Indeed, in making a description I have to use language which I didn't invent. But language is a social product. Then beyond human society there is the whole environment of the birds, the bees and the flowers, the oceans, the air and the stars. And our behavior is always in relationship to that enormous environment—just like our walking is in relation to the ground, and in relation to the form of space, object outlines and the shape of a room.

So then, the result that comes out of it, is that the more and more the scientist looks at an organism, he knows that he is not looking at an organism in an environment, he's looking at a total process, which is called "organism" *out* of its environment. But he suddenly wakes up and sees that he has a new empathy with that which he is studying. He started out to say what the organism is doing. He found that he had to paste up a few steps, and to realize that his description of the behavior of the organism involved, at the same time, a description of the behavior of the environment. So that although, unlike trees and plants, we are not rooted to the ground, but walk about fairly freely inside our bags of skins, we are nonetheless as much rooted in the natural environment as any flower or tree.

This gives us at first, as Westerners, a sense of frustration, because we say, "It sounds fatalistic." It sounds as if we were saying, "You thought you were an independent organism—you're nothing of the kind. Your environment pushes you around. But that idea simply, if we would express that idea as a result of hearing what I've just said, it would mean that we didn't understand it. You see, what was high knowledge a hundred years ago, is today common sense. And most people's common sense today is based on Newtonian mechanics. The universe is a system billiard ball of atomic events, and everybody regards his ego as an atomic event—a fundamental part, component of the universe. All right? So all these billiard balls start going clackety-clackety-clack, and knocking each other about. And so, you feel yourself to be, perhaps, one billiard ball pushed around by the world, or sometimes if you can get enough up inside that billiard ball, you can do some pushing of the world around. But mostly it pushes you.

You read B.F. Skinner, the supreme behaviorist psychologist, and he describes all phenomena of nature in terms of man being pushed around. But let's suppose that we live in a world where things don't get pushed around, and can't be pushed around. Supposing there's no puppet. Supposing there is no cause and no effect. That instead of things being pushed around, they are just happening, the way they do happen. Then you get an utterly different view, and this is the view with which we are dealing, lying behind this culture.

As I said this morning, there is no boss. You as a human being are not going to push this world around, but equally, you are not going to be pushed around by it. It goes with you. The external world goes with you, in just the same way as a back goes with a front. How would you know what you meant by "yourself," unless you knew what you meant by other. How would the sun be light, if you didn't have eyes. How would vibrations in the air be noisy, if you didn't have ears? How would rocks be hard, if you didn't have soft skin? How would they be heavy, if you didn't have muscles? It's only in relation to eyes that the sun is light. It's only in relation to a certain kind of nervous system that fire is hot. And it's only in relation to a certain musculature that rocks are heavy. So that the way you are constituted, the way your organism is formed calls into being the phenomenon of light, and sound, and weight, and color, and smell.

There is a koan in Zen Buddhism, "What is the sound of one hand?" There is a Chinese proverb that says, "One hand does not make a clap. So if two hands clap, make the clap. What is the sound of one hand?" You see, what a silly question. And yet everybody is trying to play a game in which one side will win, and there can be one hand clapping—to get rid of the opposite. Light get rid of darkness. I conquer the universe. In other words, I play the game that I am going to get one up on them, and hold my position. I am going to dominate the other. And as soon as we get into that particular kind of contest we become insane. Because what we're doing is pretending that there can be an in-group without an out-group.

Let me just give a few illustrations of this from contemporary social situations. You, or most of you here, on the whole identify yourself with the nice people. In other words, you live fairly respectable lives, and you look down upon various other people who are not nice. And there are various kinds of not-nice people.

In Sausalito, where I live, they're called "Beatniks". They are people who wear beards, and who live along the waterfront, and who don't follow the ordinary marriage customs, and who probably smoke marijuana instead of drinking alcohol, because alcohol is the drug for nice people.

What the nice people don't realize is, they need the nasty people. Think of all the conversation at dinner tables that you would miss, if you didn't have the nasty people to talk about. How would you know who you were, unless you could compare yourselves with those who are on the out? How do those in the church, who are saved, know who they are unless they have the damned. Why St. Thomas Aquinas let it out of the bag and said that in Heaven, the saints would look over the battlements of Heaven, and enjoy the just sufferings of the souls in Hell. Jolly won't it be, to watch your sister squirming down there, while you're in bliss. But, that was letting the cat out of the bag, because the in-group can't exist without the out-group.

Now in my community in Sausalito, where the out-group is sort of Beatniks, they in their turn know that they are the *real* in-group, and that up on the hill, those squares who are so dumb that they waste all their days earning money by dull work to buy pseudo-riches, such as Cadillacs and houses with mowed lawns, and wall-to-wall carpeting, which they *despise*, they feel very, very much collective ego strength by being able to talk against the squares. Because the out-group makes itself the in-group by putting the in-group in the position of an out-group. But both need the other one. This is the meaning of saying, "Love your enemies," and pray for them that despitefully use you, because you need them. You don't know who you are without the contrast. So, love your competitors, and pray for them that undercut your prices. You go together, you have a symbiotic relationship, even though it be formally described as a conflict of interest.

Now to see that kind of thing is the essence of this philosophy of nature. It goes together with the idea of the Yang and the Yin, that we don't know what the Yang is, the positive, the bright side, unless we at the same time, know what the Yin is, which is the dark side. These things define each other mutually. And to see that, you might think at first, was to settle for a view of the world that was completely static. Because after all, if white and black, good and evil, are equally pitted against one another, then so what? It all boils down to nothing.

But the universe is not arranged that way, because it has in it the principle of relativity. Now you would think, in a Newtonian and respectable Platonic universe the earth would revolve around the sun in terms of the perfect circle, but it doesn't, it's an ellipse. And if it *were* a perfect circle, the earth wouldn't revolve, because there would be no go to it. See, when you take a string with a ball on the end, and you swing it 'round your head, you don't describe a perfect circle. You know what happens? There's one moment in that swing when you have to give the thing a little charge of strength, you go whoop, whoop, whoomm, whoomm, whoomm, brrumm, brrumm,—and *that* little pulse sets the thing going. Listen to your heart. How does it go? It doesn't go "pum, pum, pum, pum, pum, pum, pum," but "pum-pum, pum-pum, pum-pum." It's got swing—it's got jazz! See?

So it seems a little off. That's why in all Chinese art, there's not symmetry. There's not complete balance between two sides of the painting, because the moment you have symmetry you have something static. But when you're a little off, then it moves. So in that way, when you study this architecture, you will see that it's always a little off. It would be dead if two sides of a room were just the same. They're always exploiting this! —Whoo, whoo, whoo, whoo, whoo.

Well now, you and they can understand this theoretically. If I say it in words, you can probably follow my meaning, and realize that all this is very true from a theoretical point of view. But what is much more important is, do we *feel* it to be so? Do we experience this relationship of man and nature to be as reliable and as true as we experience the ground under our feet, or the air coming into our lungs, or the light before our eyes? Because if we don't experience it with *that* clarity, it's not going to have any effective influence on our conduct. We'll know theoretically that we are one body with the world. The world, you might say, is your extended body. But this won't make any real difference to what you do, until you know it as surely, indeed *more* surely, than you know anything else. This amounts to a fundamental trans-formation of one's own sensation of existence - of coming to be vividly aware, if I may say so: that *you're* it!

As the Hindus say, *Tat twam asi*. You, or Thou art that. Only we feel much too guilty to agree with that. We feel that, uh, oh! that's close to madness. There are people in lunatic asylums who say that they're Jesus Christ, or that they're God. But the trouble with them is, you see, they claim this for themselves alone. They don't see that this claim goes also for anybody else. And the moment they stop making special claims, they feel lost, something crazy. But you see, if a Hindu or a Chinese person were to say, "Well, I've discovered that I'm God," this wouldn't have the same implications. People say to him rather, "Congratulations, at last you found out." Because he has an idea of God, or of ultimate reality which is not exclusive, which is not something that sets itself up as a master technician that knows all the answers.

Well, let's have a brief intermission.

2

OUT OF THE TRAP

L ast night we were getting into a kind of sticky mess, as if one had put molasses in one hand and feathers in the other, put the two together, and then started to pull off the feathers. I was pointing out that relativity is not only the human situation, but the very nature of life. It is a sort of balancing act, and rather different from the ordinary balancing act, in that the system always balances. However far out you may get to one side, life eventually comes up with the other.

But we don't perceive this for exactly the same reason that we ordinarily don't think that space is real. Most people feel that space is nothing. But when you begin to consider it carefully, you see that space and solid are relative to each other—that you cannot possibly conceive any solid body except in space. And, contrariwise, you can't conceive space except as occupied by solids. And when physicists begin to talk about properties of space—curved space, expanding space, and all that kind of thing—it at first strikes the layman as nonsensical. Thus he simply cannot conceive how nothing can have any properties.

As Einstein once said, the fish would not, of course, be aware of the water. And, in the same way, we are not aware of space as being an effective agent of some kind, as being really there.

So then, just as we think solids more real than space, so, in the same way, we give weight to positive—the Yang aspect of things, rather than Yin—the negative. And we are therefore hung up on the quest for those positive things in life: the good, the pleasurable, and so on, and think that somehow we can possess them away from, and apart from, their polar opposites. Never forget that this is not simply a case of opposition. Polarity and mere opposition are a little different in concept, because when we say that these opposites are polar, we mean that they are in fact, the abstract terms, or ends, of a sort of continuum that joins them. In the same way, the two sides of a coin are Euclidian surfaces of a solid: the coin is one; the magnet is one. But the heads and tails are different, and the north and south poles of the magnet are different. So, what you have here is the paradoxical situation of identical differences—explicitly different, but implicitly one.

OUT OF THE TRAP

We get into this situation of realizing that there isn't anything I can do to make everything always better. And, in fact, the more I try to do so, the more I am becoming blind to the relative situation, to the nature of reality. And, because I am trying to do something which, in the nature of things, is impossible, I slowly develop a feeling of chronic frustration, which is called in Buddhism, *dukkha*, usually translated as suffering, which is too imprecise. Dukkha is the chronic frustration of living in a squirrel cage where, run as you may to get out, you stay in the same place. And this is what is called, in Buddhist philosophy, *samsara*, or the Bhavachakra: *bhava* means becoming, *chakra* means wheel. And the problem that Buddhism sets is: how do we get out of the rat race? The Eternal Cycle, or to be more exact, the Everlasting Cycle, of the pursuit of one end. Pursuit of one's own end, as a matter of fact. Naturally, if you pursue your own end, you'll go round in circles.

This poses a real Gordian Knot question, because we find that we are in a circular trap. When you buy a little terrapin, and you put it on the lawn, surrounded by a ring of chicken wire, it goes around and puts it head through every hole. It goes and goes and goes, but there's no way out. So, in this fantastically difficult situation, how do we get out? Well, what of course has to be understood is that this is the wrong question. What has to be understood is that there is a trap only if someone or something is trapped. If there isn't any difference between yourself and the trap, then you are not trapped.

When we regard our experience, we always look upon it as a changing panorama of events passing before us. And we conceive that there is some constant witness, observer, ego, to whom all this happens. And this, of course, is a hallucination of the same type as the circle of fire created in the darkness by whirling a cigarette around. And, as you know, the cause of that illusion is very simply that the retinal nerve ends do not become de-activated immediately as the point of light moves. They retain, jut as a radar screen retains the image of what the rotating beam has shown. For the retina is a process that is slower than the process of the circling point of flame. Because of the relative speeds of various forms of change, the slower ones get the impression of a certain permanence.

Or, put it in another way: let's consider our experience as a route, and this includes our sensations, our feelings, our thoughts, our constant rhythm of vibrations. But in the tremendous variety and randomness of these things, there are certain constants. As, when we compose music, we will play at the basis of something a constant rhythm, as the tamboura makes a drone in Indian music, which goes on and on and on all the time. Now, in rather the same way, when we examine ribonucleic acid, we find a chain of molecular particles in a certain order, and that order repeats, so that you have a chain of a certain kind. So, in the same way, the total order of experience repeats certain things, and this repetition gives us memory, and gives us the clue that this particular stream has a signature. As in music, there may be certain phrases that are constantly repeated, however elaborated, for there may be variations on the theme, but always at the basis of it there is this repetitious regularity.

Because of that, we get the sensation that there is a constant observer of the panorama. And then, as that becomes more and more a fixed impression, we attempt to use this observer, or by being this observer, to exercise an influence on the stream from a point, as it were, virtually outside the stream. And it's this that sets up frustration.

We get this when we try, under the influence of schooling and parents, to alter our feelings. When we feel guilty for hating our mothers, or something of that kind, or hating someone at all, we say to ourselves: "You shouldn't hate." But you do. You say: "You should love." But you don't. And, obviously, if you make a great effort to love somebody whom you don't love, then there is always detectable a kind of phoniness in your attitude. And loving people by force creates resentment and hostility in both parties.

If you love someone, or rather you manifest what would be called loving actions out of nothing but a sense of duty, the person whom you love in that way feels deprived. He feels that your heart isn't really in it, because you are being dishonest with your own feelings. But this is the kind of mockery that comes up when we are inwardly split into the thinker on one side—the thoughts on the other; the feeler on one side—and the feelings on the other.

There are various ways in which this split can be described and there are ways in which we can discuss how it arises. I gave you one: the regular rhythm pattern. Being, as it were, abstracted from the main stream, and made a separate constant. Another is perhaps simpler to understand, which is that, as we think, thinking is a process of symbolization. Among all the things for which we have symbols, we have one for I, one for ourselves, one for this organism, this center of awareness. And this symbol becomes, like so many symbols, confused with what it represents, as we confuse money with wealth. And, because of that, we try to perform operations with the symbol, which would be like trying to do something with an hour. You know, we say: "What are you going to do with your time?" As if you could do something with time! The time is simply a form of measurement, and trying to do something with time is like eating inches. Very frustrating, indeed!

So, as a result of this confusion, we again get the sensation of there being an observer. But the funny thing is: we can never find it. Do what you will to track down this observer—it's never there. The tail retreats as fast as you follow it.

Now, on the other hand, if we think in gestalt terms, if we think in terms of figure and ground, you would be inclined to feel that there is some continuum or medium in which experience occurs. Just, in the same way, that when you listen to the radio, you're hearing sounds, but all those sounds are on the diaphragm in the speaker: the sounds do not proclaim the diaphragm—they don't say anything about it. That's taken for granted. The announcer does not announce at the beginning of the day: "Ladies and gentlemen, from now on all the sounds that you hear out of this instrument are in fact vibrations of the diaphragm in the speaker." And therefore, just as we ignore space and think of it as nothing, we could perfectly well ignore the continuum in which experience is occurring. But, if so, that continuum does not have the same sort of relationship to what is going on in it as does the observer to the observed. Because the observer to the observed is a function of memory—the repetition. And the memory is not the continuum. It's still vibrations in it. So if there is something underlying the changing panorama of experience, it is of course completely unthinkable, undefinable. We cannot state anything about it at all. But that does not however mean that it's impossible to realize its presence, in some other form than what we would call ordinary experience, and yet, at the same time, not really separate from ordinary experience. This would add, therefore, to our awareness of everything a kind of new dimension, and we'd have great difficulty in pointing it out, because it isn't hidden.

You can always point out things that are hidden, but it's very difficult to point out something that everybody's looking at and doesn't see.

Take a very simple illustration. Let us suppose that you have been brought up to think of the moon as simply a plate, a flat disk in the sky. Then one day somebody woke up and realized it was a ball. He would have great difficulty pointing this out to other people, just as we had great difficulty in convincing people that the world was round, or that the stars were not supported above us in crystal spheres.

In this sense then, the dimension of the moon, once you see it, is perfectly clear. But if you don't see it, you can't be talked into it. So, in exactly the same way, there is this dimension of everyday life which isn't different from everyday life, from everyday consciousness, but we just haven't caught onto it.

Now, let's experiment a bit with this. Let's go back to the fundamental point: that there isn't anything you can do to "up" yourself. And if you consider that, you feel sort of stuck. So I would say at this point: Never mind. So you're stuck. Therefore, you might say that you just have to accept the way it is right now.

But that isn't saying enough. Or maybe it's saying too much. Supposing you don't accept the way things are right now? Well, that's the same thing going along too. So, therefore, watch what you're doing very carefully. You can get down to the sensation of what I would call the flow of experience. It's going along... it's in the sound of my voice... it's in the sound of the wind... it's in everything your eyes see as you look around. And here it is, flowing along.

Now, what I'm saying is: That's it. I really don't know what I mean by that, except: Watch it. That's it. And if you find yourself not watching it, or, for example, resisting it, that's it too.

Just let happen what happens, even if that includes resistance to what is happening. Now watch yourself carefully as you do that. You see, we are not looking for any result; We are here and now. But, if you are looking for a result; if you are in a state of expectation: watch that. And follow it. You can't make a mistake, whatever you do.

This is the same process as learning to ride a bicycle. Because whichever way you fall, to the left or to the right, you turn the wheel into the way you're falling. It's the same thing that pilots learn in flying planes. And they get to a point where they say, well, the plane flies itself, and it really does, if you get your hands on the wheel of a good plane, it flies itself. So, in the same way, as you follow like this the flow of existence, you find that it functions by itself. It does.

At first, then, you may get this rather strange, passive feeling that this is happening to me. "It is happening to me." As you watch what goes on, you won't discover any "me" separate from the flow that you're watching. You'll realize if anything is "you", it's That.

Now, I hope you can follow this. You could do it in a certain way: by simply listening to *all* the sound that's going on, only I would say "hearing" rather than "listening"-as one can "see" distinct from "looking", as it were. Allow your ears to hear anything they want to hear. Simply let these eardrums vibrate to any available sound. And in exactly the same way as you do that, let your mind think whatever it wants to think. And go with it. Go with the flow of thought. You will see that after a while it is impossible not to go with it, because even your resistance to it is part of the thought stream, and that's still going along with itself. When you discover that the resistance, too, is part of the stream—you will see that it was redundant to say "go with it"—there's no one separate from it to go with it.

The same thing applies exactly in the consideration of the passage of time. What we are doing at the moment is that we've brought our attention to bear on the flow of experience as it is now. And in this sort of consideration, this sort of contemplation, you get the feeling of being in the present, watching what is going on. Only, momentarily, your thoughts may concern themselves with the past or the future. You may be concerned about something that's going to happen, and instead of listening fully to the sound of my voice, you're entering thoughts about tomorrow. Maybe you'll check that, you see, and say: "No, I shouldn't do that, I should come back to 'now'." But the same principle applies exactly as turning the wheel of the bicycle: if you fall into the past—turn that way; if you fall into the future—turn that way. Because your consideration of the past is happening now, as is also your consideration of the future. So that just as you cannot not go with the stream, you cannot get out of the present. There is nowhere else to be.

At first, the situation I am describing when I say "you cannot" sounds like a limitation, a bondage. "I am trapped. I cannot get out of this." But don't you see that what you are first of all describing as the trap is precisely the condition of freedom? If you insist that you're trapped by the present, by the existing flow of thought, the way it is, or the existing flow of experience, then of course you will resent it. When you discover that you *are* it, and the reason that you can't get away from it is that it *is* you,—this is a very different state of affairs. There is no trap. You are the process. It's not happening to you. You're not its victim. It's *you*. So then, instead of asking, "How shall I get out of it", that question simply disappears.

Let me go back and approach that point from another angle. If you say: "I want to get out of it"—when you want something, you pretty much know what you want, but people when they're really challenged on what sort of domain they would like to get into other than this one, they can only talk a little way ahead. But if they follow through that wish to be in some different kind of existence, they find it difficult to picture it. Because they see it would always lead around to the same place that they are now, eventually. This is the truth underlying, say, the idea that suicide is no escape, because however intolerable a situation may be, the only way out is *into* the center, not *away*.

And so it is only by, as we must state it because of the limitations of language, at first "going with" whatever the experience is. Now, supposing the situation is horrible. I cannot accept it in the sense of "liking it", because the situation includes a pain (maybe), and aggravating the pain by my extremely strong objections to it. Those objections are just as much a part of the whole scene as the pain. In fact, they're really inseparable. The pain is not pain unless you object to it.

So, if you say to yourself: "Something is going to happen which I dread very much, and, really, if I were a spiritually superior human being, I ought not to dread it"—that's really creating fantasy. You must allow yourself to dread it. You must allow yourself quite freely to worry, because it's okay.

When I say, "it's okay", it's like saying, "Well, that's it, too." And we don't really know what we mean by this, except that when I say, "That's it", that means: "Keep watching." Keep your mind on the mark - that's real concentration. Not just staring at something. Real concentration is like following music, dancing to music, something like that. It isn't being all tied up in a knot with your mind hypnotized like a chicken with its head to a chalk line.

It's this constant "flowing with", only to discover that you *are* the stream. And therefore there is no problem about flowing with it. You can't do anything else. But that is a statement of freedom, as distinct from a statement of bondage.

So you're your own trap. And if you want to bite yourself with its teeth, it's a free country. You can do that. That's the game of hide-and-seek, pretending that the trap is different from you. "Being trapped"—see if you can get out! Because, you see, that's what people do interminably. What do people spend their time with— why, with puzzles. You say, "We've got to kill time for awhile",... what do you do?—you read a mystery story. That's a puzzle, a "whodunit". Or you do a crossword puzzle. Or you play a game. You always set yourself a problem, and then work it out. Well, that's what everyone is doing. They set themselves a problem, and then they work it out. Now we've set ourselves a whopper.

Now, what happens? For a moment, you were watching this flow going along, this flow of experience. But then you find, a few minutes later, you're off on something else. You're sort of distracted, without realizing that this distraction is perfectly okay too. Why did you leave the point? Well, obviously because you wanted to. Because you get what you want. And I'm amazed that all of us rather like being restless. It's very interesting working in a meditation session: you'll often find that after a period of meditation, the director will say, "All right, now, everyone can rest." I suddenly caught myself doing this one day, and I said instead, "Okay, everyone, return to your normal state of restlessness."

Yet, you see, that normal state of restlessness can't be fought. If you put it down, all you'll do is you'll stir it up. And so you simply must allow yourself to be restless. But you will see that as soon as you do that, that brings a dimension of consciousness into it that wasn't there before. You're aware of this constantly restless state and, being aware of it, you ask the question, "Is that really the way I want to be?" If you do, you do; if you don't, then you don't.

But if you fight it, it'll back up, just like trying to go fast through the water on a ship with a blunt prow: You'll back it all up against you. So there is a way of not fighting yourself. And even when you're trying to fight yourself—don't fight with that.

Now, if we talk about this, we go on and on and on, like children playing "hand over hand". And we can say: Accept it the way it is; and if you don't accept the way it is, accept that. And if you can't do that - accept that. Whenever you get into this sort of infinite regression you are on a circular course. That "haven't-we-been-here-before" feeling develops after awhile. It is exactly the circular course which indicates that what you are either trying to catch on the one hand, or what you're trying to run away from on the other hand, is the fellow that's doing the running. That's what the circular course means. And the moment you discover that, and you know that—the chase stops. Only the chase won't stop while there's the slightest thought that what you're pursuing is not the pursuer. Or that what you're fleeing is not the fleer.

Well, you may want to bring the intellect to bear on that, for the simple reason that that seems a rather outrageous statement to some people. They say, "Do you mean that everything that's happening to me, including everything going on in the outside world, is myself?" Well, indeed it is. But of course not in the ordinary way in which we use the word "myself", meaning the ego. But, in a very real sense, which we can demonstrate in all kinds of ways, biologically...neurologically... physically, the separation (to talk about it in purely physical terms) of the body from the outside world isn't a separation at all. It's true: there is a boundary of human skin which we take to be the point of separation. But that is a hallucination because, to begin with, the organism and, as a matter of fact, anything whatsoever, has the same sort of properties as a flame. Now really, there is hardly such a thing as a flame. Consider a candle with a flame on it. We see that bright little leaf-shaped piece of light, the fire, and say, "a flame". It would be more correct to say, "a flaming", because that is a stream of hot gas, and no gas stays put in it. If it did, there wouldn't be a flame.

In just the same way, everything that exists is a stream. But we can see it as a wriggle or a whirlpool in the stream. But, as everything is flowing through, there is certainly no fixed distinction between the outside and the inside. And, of course, biologically we know that the skin itself is an osmotic membrane: that is to say, a connector of the body with the environment, full of tubes and extraceptors, nerve-ends which are simply communicating constantly the flow of vibration on the outside of the skin to the inside of the skin. Think about it a little more and you'll realize that you couldn't have an inside without an outside. Here is the same reciprocity, the same thing that we get between all the opposites, between front and back and everything else. The self—the sensation of self—or, I would say, the sensation of here and now, goes with "other", that is to say, the sensation of "there" and "then".

You cannot possibly conceive the meaning of *now* without the meaning of *then*... of *here* without *there*... or *self* without *other*. And this inseparability of concepts reveals the hidden conspiracy between now and then, of the eternity, shall we say, of which now and then are the polar aspects...the omnipresence of which here and there are polar aspects... the Brahman of which self and other are polar aspects.

We cannot name or describe the unity between the poles, because all description is a matter of putting things in boxes; it's classification - pigeon-holing. And when you pigeon-hole things, you ask, "Is you is or is you ain't?"... "Do you belong in this box or don't you? Either you belong in it or you don't. There's no other place for you to go. Either you're an elephant or you're a non-elephant. And everything that's not an elephant belongs in the box for non-elephants." But what is it that is in common between elephants and non-elephants? What is in common between the box and the outside of the box? Why, obviously, the boundary of the box belongs both to the box and to what's outside the box. It's the outside of the box and the inside of the non-box. They share this wall—it belongs to both of them. It is held in common.

In other words, the dividing line is held in common by what it divides. It belongs to both of them. It unites them. It makes them identical differences. So, in that sense then, what happens *to* you, *is* you.

"But," you say, "it's not what I want. It's not what I will. It makes no difference what I do in my head as to whether the wind blows now or not. It's not in my control." Well, nor is your metabolism... and is that you, or isn't it? That *happens*. What about your volition? I choose to talk or not to talk. It seems that way, but on the other hand, I am damned if I know how I do this thing called talking. When I really go into it, it *happens*. Only, I've got a sort of proprietary sense on it... I've labelled it "mine". I do seem to have control, choice, selection. But, if I think down into that, you see, I don't see how it works. It's fantastic that I can make a noise, or even raise a hand. I don't know how it happens. How do you decide? How do you manage to be conscious? How do you manage to make an effort. Nobody knows—you just do it. which is another way of saying, "It just happens."

Now, imagine then getting the sensation of something you're not used to: that everything that goes on in the outside world, is also *you*. And it's what you're doing. That's spooky. See, that's the same feeling you get when you are learning to ride the bicycle—it "happens". And you feel as if you were suddenly in charge of an enormously powerful automobile, as if something's running away with you.

Somehow, I find that I'm in control of it by *not* being in control of it—like the plane flying itself. Now this is so strange that it sends some people crazy. And they get up and announce that they are God Almighty, which is what Jung calls inflation. And you must watch out for inflation if you're in the habit of encouraging mystical experiences. Because, if you're not experienced in what I call "spiritual know-how", and the only kind of religious background you have is Judaeo-Christian, you naturally will discover that you're God. But in the Judaeo-Christian tradition, God means "the Boss of the Universe", and is therefore worshipped under the symbol of kingship, the royal father of the world. And therefore, since kingship is exclusive, if you say, "I am God", and start letting it be known to your fellow men that you are the king, you'll be playing "I'm the king of the castle"... "Get down, you dirty rascal."

But, you see, if you're properly educated about mystical experience, you will realize that mystical experience isn't really allowed in Christianity. There are Christian mystics, but they get by because they really watch their language. They walk a very, very risky tightrope. They're always in grave danger of falling into hideous heresy, or pantheism. And Christians are afraid of pantheism because, as I have pointed out, it's democracy in the kingdom of heaven. Everyone's God. And this, to a tyrannical form of government, is an intolerable suggestion.

If you think of all this in terms of quite a different mythology, say, Hindu mythology or Buddhist mythology, this problem then of inflation doesn't arise, or at least not so easily. You can, of course, give yourself airs and graces of being a Buddha, being a great rishi, or something like that, but society doesn't resent that so intensely as it resents the claim to be in personal charge of the whole universe.

Lots of people in insane asylums get this sensation, and nobody knows what to do about them, because psychiatrists as a rule don't know anything about the mystical experience. You may be sure, as a matter of fact, with certain exceptions, psychiatry, as we know it today, particularly the psychiatry of mental hospitals, the army, prisons, and many ordinary practitioners, will define any state of consciousness that is not quite usual as psychotic. It doesn't matter much what it is. There is a research worker at Langley Porter, who has been making electro-encephalograms of people in a state of meditation, and they get a different kind of alpha rhythm from other people. They find that they can control their alpha rhythm. When these electroencephalograms are shown to most psychiatrists, and they are not told under what circumstances they were made, they will look at this and say, "Hmm...there's pathology there." Because you will find similar alpha rhythms in some pathological cases, as in catatonics: you see, they're very withdrawn and quiet.

So, official psychiatry is a frantic paranoia, a frantic concern with preserving the consensus of what reality is. Reality is what you read in the newspaper... reality is, you know, "facing facts." Any experience different from that, particularly when any kind of religious significance is attached to it, will automatically be called psychotic. If you ever get mixed up with a mental hospital, never, never say a word about religion. Because according to most psychoanalysts, to official psychoanalysis, religion is a delusional system anyway, and this feeling is widely prevalent in that particular profession, although I must acknowledge the exceptions. You see, that's always what lies behind the fear of what we used to call as children, "religious mania." You know, the little old ladies who cluster around the church, and are always in and out—we call them religious maniacs. And the ultimate extreme of religious mania is to proclaim oneself to be Jesus Christ. And so this is something to watch out for, this sort of inflationary situation that comes as soon as you see that the inside world and the outside world go together—are a single field, or process, or whatever you want to call *It*.

3

YOGA CARA

So then, we're continuing with the subject of Mahayana Buddhism. And, in the last seminar I discussed almost entirely, the school of Mahayana, which is known as *Madyamica* in Sanskrit—this word meaning, approximately, "the middle way."

Madyamica has been called, in the best books on the subject, the central philosophy of Buddhism, and is not, what we call in the West, a philosophy at all. It's a method for changing your state of consciousness. In other words, it's not a system of ideas such as propounded by Plato, or Kant, or Hegel. It's a dialectical method. That is to say, dialectic being in the sense of a discourse between a teacher and a student, the purpose of which is not to explain or inculcate a certain set of ideas, but to change one's basic state of feeling, that is to say, to change the sensation that you have of your own existence.

All Buddhism is concerned with this. The very crux of Buddhism, the thing which is called *Bodhi*, b-o-d-h-i, which means, "awakening". It comes from the same root as the word Buddha: *B-o-d-h*, Bodh, or *B-u-d-h*, Budh, is "to know," but better, it is "to be awake."

Some of you have probably exposed yourself to the teachings of Giurdjieff, a wonderful old rascal, who used to give lectures in which he would keep completely silent for a while, and get everybody embarassed, and you know, they were all expecting something to happen, and he would look individually at everybody in the group, and when everybody was feeling awkward, he would say, "*Wake Up!*" "You're all asleep, and if you don't wake up, I won't give any lecture." And this is a very good attitude, actually.

Zen, as you know, uses sharp tactics of various kinds, and the whole idea then, is that a person who is under illusion (Maya), thinks of himself basically as a victim, someone caught in a trap, someone subject to fate, the will of God, or whatever you want to call it, who got involved in life passively. That's why I use the word, "victim", and he has, therefore, the sensation of his consciousness as being a kind of passive, but nevertheless very delicate and tender receptor, or participant of everything that goes on, so that life in general occurs to you—it happens to you, and there's nothing you can do about it.

And you say, "Well, it's awful. I can't get myself out of this trap." So, the technique of the philosophical dialogue that I was describing as Madyamica is to get you to drop your defenses. In other words, you can discover as practically a physical sensation, that you tend to be on the defensive all the time. You are exerting, through every muscle practically, a resistance against the world, all of which is excessive. You do need a certain resistance, you need a certain muscular tonus, but your body does that for you. You don't need to will it.

It's like if you lie on the floor and relax, you don't need to do anything to hold yourself together, the floor will hold you up, and your skin will keep you inside. But most people are actually doing things to hold themselves together, even in this situation of complete relaxation, because they don't really trust their own life. And that is the lack of trust in one's own life, the perpetual attitude of defensiveness, it is a result of a kind of mis-feeling of one's own existence, as being something alien to the universe that endures, as I said, and is simply a passive recipient of experience.

So then, the whole process of a therapeutic dialogue which was invented by this marvelous man, Nagajuna—in the following of the Buddha—(It's a strange thing that the Buddha was very, very creative towards other people. That is to say, the basic idea of Buddhism does *not* preclude other people being just as much Buddha as Buddha was.)

There's a little difficulty in Christianity about this, you see. Everybody harps back to the Christ as the unique and only incarnation of God, and so He's on a very special pedestal which nobody else is ever allowed to climb up on, and this, of course, makes the teaching and work of Jesus completely ineffective. But Buddhism has the advantage, they never did that: so that Nagajuna, who could come later than Buddha was in a way a wiser man than the Buddha himself. But only because he stood on the shoulders of Buddha and carried the Buddha's dialogue to, not it's full conclusion, but to a full conclusion.

We can go further today, you see, this thing hasn't stopped at all. It isn't something that we go back to as a past and say, "Well, we're going to tell you all about a thing called Buddhism, which is a fixed body of practices and beliefs, in which certain people in Asia believe, and if you're interested, you can believe in it, too." It's not like that at all! It's an activity that is going on, and when it gets mixed up in the context of Western Civilization, western science, western technology—it will do things that the Asian people never dreamed of, and might not approve of.

So, it's very important in approaching this—this is one of our difficulties you see. If I were a lecturer on Buddhism in the context of the academic world, I would have to observe certain game rules. That is to say, I would have to discuss the subject as entirely historical—as something of the past. And I would be expected to give you extremely accurate information about what it was, what other people thought, and what they did.

The moment that I began to suggest that this thing had any vitality to it, and might have some effect on you, I would be ruled out as academically unrespectable. They would say, "This man is no longer qualified to be a professor, because he is advocating these things, and not taking an objective point of view to it." You see, it's very funny—all obsolete subjects are studied by the historical method. So, if you study in the university religion, it comes under the heading of the history of religions. For the same reason, the introductory course in philosophy is usually the History of Philosophy. Just imagine, teaching children mathematics with the introductory course being the History of Mathematics, so that they would start doing sums in Egyptian and Roman numerals, and going through all the procedures that ancient man went through to arrive at modern mathematics. In the first course of medicine, they proceed immediately to practical matters, the most up-to-date knowledge of human physiology, and they teach that—only when you become a graduate school student in the history of medicine, do you run across an elective course in the history of medical science? So, this way of putting everything at a distance of history is a way of castrating it, making it completely ineffective, so that it won't do anything anymore.

So that's why I cannot work in the academic world, because, although I know their game rules, and how to study Buddhism from the historical method—when you get involved in that, after a while nobody's interested and it becomes completely boring. You can acquire a huge library, and you can go into the facts endlessly, and then what? But the one thing that the academicians can console themselves with, is the one thing they're very much afraid of—a teacher of religion who's out to convert people. Because that, you see, is imposing upon you a particular, individual, and subjective point of view. So if, in other words, a person who is teaching Christianity should start preaching from his academic chair, instead of just saying what Christians did and so on, in such and such a period—they would be very frightened of that.

The advantage a Buddhist has, is that he has no opinions that he is trying to put over on you. He's only trying to help you get rid of your opinions. That is to say, to get rid of any fixed view of the world, and of yourself—because we use what are called views, in Sanskrit: *drish-ti*, as methods of clinging to existence. So, there is something that is called in Sanskrit, *sa-kaya-dris-ti*, which means "the view of separateness." The view of your being, this thing that I was talking about—the separate, the insular recipient of experience.

Say, you have feelings. But, the language we speak compels you to say *you* have feelings, as if *you* were something on the one hand, and your *feelings* were something else on the other. You have thoughts, as if the thinker stands on the one hand and inspects thoughts on the other. So, that one has a view of life in which there is a panorama of thoughts, of feelings, of sensations going along constantly, but one can say constantly because of the impression that *you* are distinct from them, standing aside from them as the constant inspector of the procession. You get the feeling that you endure, but precariously, threatenedly, while the procession of thoughts and feelings goes on by you.

Now you can very easily see that this is the result of the memory process, which gives the illusion of constancy in the flow, and, therefore, in the same way as the famous old Buddhist analogy, that when you rotate a burning brand in the darkness, you give the illusion of a continuous circle of fire because of the memory of the retina, where the impression of the spark doesn't fade out immediately, but lingers. And so, as you see this thing in front of your eyes, it seems to form a circle, whereas there is no circle. There is only a moment, an instant of flame. So Buddhists argue, there is only this moment. And actually, you, who come in at the door are not the same people who are sitting here. Just as in the whirlpool of water, there is no constant water, there is only going on a continuous behavior, whirling in the water—but no water stays in it. So, in exactly the same way, you who came into the door a few minutes ago, and are now sitting here, are entirely different, only you are clinging to the idea of your continuity.

Actually, there is only the moment, the instant, what is called in Sanskrit, the *ksana*, life is instantaneous. And if you see that, you get a kind of a new angle on St.

Paul's famous pronouncement that we shall all be changed in a moment, in a twinkling of an eye, on the morning when the last trumpet sounds. You see, the Christian has put everything into chronology—that there is going to be a thing called the Last Day, and a trumpet of the angels is going to awaken the dead.

The trumpet's sounding now, you see, for the Buddhists. Wake up! There is this moment! And this is eternity. Only you are stringing the moments together, and you are creating time out of eternity. You are wondering, you are identifying yourself, in other words, with all the things that have happened to me. And you're worrying about all the things that will. But actually, you are never anywhere but now. This is a very interesting discipline, that is given in all systems of Yoga and Buddhist meditation. The student is told to live in the present completely, to never relax awareness of what you are doing now. Be here. So you would say in the ordinary way, I have thoughts about tomorrrow and yesterday, I'm distracted, my mind doesn't stay focused on the present. That's the way it seems, yes.

What you do instead is, you try to focus your attention completely on the present. You find this a very difficult thing to do because you don't know when the present is. In other words, you don't recognize that anything happens until it's already a memory. It has, as it were, to be in your consciousness long enough to make an impression. And you say, well, in looking at this table, (I wish I could find something different from tables to give illustrations from, all lecturers are always talking from tables.) In looking at this pipe, I don't know that it's here until somehow, or other, it has lingered. So, I ask, "Am I actually knowing the present pipe, or is it always past?"

As you continue to practice this exercise, you get the funny feeling that your memory of something past is also a present event. You see? You have the memory, it is already here, and this begins to bug you, like it did St. Augustine. He couldn't understand memory—he got into a terrrible tailspin about it. Because, you see, the memory of the past is something always present. So, you finally realize the whole exercise you're undertaking was pointless, because there is nowhere else to be but the present.

That was the point in trying to make you do this thing—to get you to realize that there is no past, and there is no future. There is only now, and you *can't* get out of it. So, relax, you're in eternity, in the moment. And this flows along, or flows, or doesn't flow, you know this thing of Tennyson's poem, "Such a tide of moving seems to sleep, to full for sound or foam?" The unmoved mover. The idea of somehow, motion and stillness going together. Activity and peace. The eye of the hurricane. You see, everything is really like that.

Well, now, all that I've said hitherto in introductory, to going on to this seminar, to discuss the second great point of view that is involved in Mahayana Buddhism. The first, the Madyamica, the middle way, was, as I said, to destroy all your hang-ups, fixed opinions about the nature of life so that you don't use ideas, beliefs, religious prejudices, preferences, opinions. You don't use them to cling. It demolishes every idea of reality that you could have. That's Madyamica, that's Nagajuna. Now, a little later in time, there arose in India, two other great Buddhist philosophers, respectively, Asanga, and Vasubandhu, and they have been two Vasubandhus, either father and son, or teacher and student, who took his teacher's name, and they lived in this vague dating that we have. It's impossible to pin it down, about 400 A.D.

They are responsible for what is called the *Yoga Cara* school, sometimes called also, the *Gnatimatra*, which means, "The School of Consciousness Only." And, it looks deceptively like what we call in Western philosophy, Subjective Idealism, as taught, say, by Berkeley or Bradley. That, in other words, the only reality is your mind. As this is propounded in Western philosophy—everything that exists is in your mind. You know an external world only in your mind. You know the sense of space between yourself and something distant from you. That is a mental phenomenon. And so, it could be argued that your mind alone exists, and that all that you see is an imagination.

The extreme way of posing this is the doctrine called "Solipscism," that there is only yourself, and that everything else is your dream. There has never been any way of disproving this, except my idea, which I think almost disproves it, that I would like to present at a conference of Solipscists, where they argue as to which one of them is the one that is really there. So, the point of view, of say, Berkeley or Bradley, in the Western tradition of Subjective Idealism, is not solipscistic. But it is that everybody has a certain independent existence, but as a mind. And that all particular minds are, as it were, minds in a super mind, which is the mind of God.

The Western philosopher has, therefore, dealt with the problem, "Does something exist when there's nobody around to look at it?" by saying, "*There was a young man, who said, 'God, I find it exceedingly odd, that a tree, as tree, simply ceases to be when there's no-one around in the quad.' 'Young man, your aston-ishment's odd, I'm always around in the quad, so the tree, as a tree, never ceases to be, since observed by yours faithfully, God.'*"

But, this isn't the same point of view that we're going to deal with in Oriental philosophy, because we start from completely different assumptions as to the nature of mind and matter. You see, if you don't get those straight, you confuse the Yoga Cara school with Subjective Idealism. Unfortunately, Professor Tako-kusu, in his book, *The Essentials of Buddhist Philosophy*, uses Western school names to classify the different types of Buddhist philosophy—uses, you know, Nihilism, Subjective Idealism, etc., all down the line, and this is very confusing. Because when you start with the basic idea of what is Mind, you don't begin with the opposition that we begin with, which is Mind/Matter. You begin instead with the contrast, Mind and Form. Form is furthermore broken down into Name and Form. It is called in Sanskrit, *Nama Rupa*, name-form. And this stands, in their system, as distinct from the idea of matter meaning "stuff" in our common sense.

We begin with this break, that we have the notion that there is some kind of heavy, hard substance, and this substance is energized by spiritual forces, which, just as the potter turns clay into pots, the spiritual forces take hold of the unintelligent stuff of matter, and weave it into all the various shapes of life. And so, then, when we die, here is a person, you see, that is going along, talking, chatting, doing his business everyday, and suddenly: zingo! his body lies there. Where is he? What's happened to him?

Of course, the mind has left, and there lies only the stuff. So, we've got this idea in our minds of the energy, which is something impalpable, something un-stuff, you see, animating or not animating something that is heavy, and hard and dusty. Now that great contrast comes, of course, from the book of Genesis, from the idea that the Lord, God, formed to the world out of some clay. Adam was a clay figurine.

This idea is not in the same way in Hindu thought, but something deceptively like it is in Hindu thought, which causes the confusion. For example, Shankir, who is the great interpreter of the Upanishads, in the tradition of interpretation which is called the Advita Vedanta, the non-dual vedanta, sometimes uses the symbol of gold and things made of gold which sounds like the pots and the clay, but he uses it in another way than we do. Whereas we use the clay as the symbol for the stuff out of which things are made, and which is inferior because the shape, being spiritual, is more important than the stuff— he uses it in exactly the opposite way. All beings are of the nature of the divine, just as many different objects can be made out of gold. It is all one gold, though the shape may change, and he describes the shape as ephemeral and impermanent, but it is the gold which is the thing that endures.

Do you see, that's using the analogy, the metaphor, in exactly the opposite way than the way we use clay, or stuff, and form in the West? So then, you don't have at the basis of the mind-only philosophy, a conception of mind, which is the kind of impalpable spook presiding over the hard and heavy stuff. You have to begin somewhere else all together. And this is the fascination of studying Oriental culture. You have to re-adjust your own common sense to get at it. What on earth do these people mean? Especially when I don't really have any words in my own language into which I can translate their ideas.

Fortunately, it isn't all that inaccessible, because what we have here is not merely words, if that were all, we would be absolutely lost - we have the techniques, the meditation disciplines, which you can use, and through using them, find out what it was that they meant, experimentally.

So then, we start basically with the fundamental word that is used in Sanskrit for the activity of mind, *citta*. We Romanize this as *c-i-t-t-a*, the root, *c-i-t* is basic to mind. Now the Sanskrit language has many words for mind. We've got this one word: mind, which sort of has to take care of everything. We've got intellect, we've got vision, consciousness, and so on, but they're all very vague in the way their used. Sanskrit is quite precise. But *cit* is the basic term. And reality, itself, is called in vedant philosophy *Sat-cit-ananda*. *Sat* means, "real". This word, the root *sa* in Sanskrit is, what is manifest and is really there. It comes from breathing out. You make the sound, *sa*. And so, it's really there.

Cit is, it is conscious, has the quality of consciousness, *ananda* means bliss. Because reality if not blissful, would not be. The game has to be worth the candle, or it would stop. If the fundamental energy and impulse of the universe were not blissful, the whole system would have ceased long ago. Even if it involves pain, this pain is masochistic. That is to say, it is pain being enjoyed fundamentally as a pleasure. Like you can have a grievance, and make your whole life a cause around your grievance, by being a professionally rejected woman, or a failure of some kind, and you can really build this up into a big thing. And so, in this funny sort of rather trivial human way, you make an ecstasy out of suffering. The idea here is that the universe is fundamentally, insofar as it involves suffering, making an ecstasy out of it. That is to say, that every element of pain, in the whole scheme of things, is the necessary, what will I call it, contrasting element that you need in order to bring out the fundamental exuberance and joy of being, that you wouldn't know. In other words, that you were here unless something stopped you.

Mind in this philosophy, what is meant by *cit*, is practically exactly the same thing as we mean by existence. When we use the word being, in order to, for example, when Dr. Johnson heard of Berkeley's philosophy that everything existed only in your mind, his response was to kick a stone—as if to demonstrate, "That's the real world!" But it is exactly this sense of "humph" that is meant by *cit*.

That's why, when a Zen master would be asked, "What is the fundamental meaning of Buddhism?"— "Ha-a!" You know, this thing, this sense of impact—that is what it is. In other words, mind, in this philosophy, is as concrete as you can imagine. And so it is called, and we, in a future seminar, will go into this from another point of view, the word: *Vagra*, which means diamond, is used for it, because the diamond is simultaneously the hardest thing there is, and the most transparent. There's a whole philosophy of Buddhism worked around the diamond. So what you've got here, you see, is a conception of mind, which instead of being the impalpable ghostly thing that we have had, is the most intensely tough reality, adamantine mind. Bang! Hard! You. Here. You see, this very strong sense of being. So the philosophy of "it's all in your mind," has to be hung on *this* as distinct from being hung on something flimsy and impalpable. Now we're going to have an intermission.

4

THE PSYCHOLOGY OF MYSTICAL EXPERIENCE

I have throughout all my life been a disciple of William James, who, as you may know, wrote a book called *The Varieties of Religious Experience*. I have always been fascinated by James' approach to this subject because it involves a way in which we might understand the dynamics of various people's differing accounts of their visions of God, and of their place in the universe. Sometimes these visions sound very different: some people seem to experience God as extremely far-out and others, as something "up there" to be venerated, adored, and obeyed; but other people seem to experience God as something completely inside, as something that is the essence of what, when you really come down to it, you call yourself. And so it seems that there is a conflict between these two forms of experience. But I am very suspicious about these varied accounts because I am not so sure that they aren't two different forms of the same thing, described in different kinds of language.

Speaking from another domain of experience, some people will describe a pain as a cold sting, while others will describe it as a hot pang—because very, very cold is pain, and very, very hot is pain; but when it comes right down to it, both are the same kind of pain.

Then there are other extremes of human experience, such as ecstasy. Think of absolute pleasure. It is said that when a French girl who is really on to it, is being made love to, she will exclaim, "Kill me, kill me!" to her man. Thus, we can describe ecstasy in the language of pleasure, and we can describe it in the language of pain. There is a domain where pleasure and pain meet, such that we weep for joy and shudder with delight. And by this sort of reasoning I seek to unify the quarrels between religions. On the one hand, I will as eagerly sit in meditation with Buddhists, where they cross their legs and look exactly like the image of their venerated being, the Buddha; or on the other hand, I will, like the Christians, Jews, or Muslims, bow before the unseen, transcendent presence, I will go with either one. What this entire argument really comes down to, and what I think is of vital interest to every one of us, is that we are presently, and uncomfortably, aware of being alive at the end of time— in what the Hindus call *Kali Yuga*. Things are running down, and time is running out. We are haunted by an insuperable set of problems—over-population, pollution, the nuclear bomb, irreconcilable political conflicts—and everyone of us has the sense, the haunting feeling, that these problems cannot be solved, and that probably we have only about thirty or so more years of life on this planet.

Of course, this may not be so. We may muddle through. But the fact of the matter remains that within zero to seventy years from now, all of us will be dead anyway. And we all know this. It is a recurrent, disturbing thought in the back of our minds: the end— and then what? We all have to face it. We are all going to evaporate, and turn into bones and dust. But now, I look at this problem with complete fascination. So, instead of avoiding this, or looking the other way and saying, "Oh well, later," let's look at it.

What would it be like to go to sleep and never wake up? Every child thinks about this. But philosophers disdain the question. They say, "Oh, that's a meaningless speculation. You're just using words." But for a child, who is an essential person, it is vey real to think about this. So, lets face facts. Let us not dream of reincarnation or of *deva chan* or of worlds beyond, but let us suppose that it is very real that when you're dead, you're dead, and that you are never going to wake up again.

Well, I scratch my head and think, "That isn't going to be like going into the dark forever, because darkness is something I can imagine. And it's not going to be like being buried alive, it is going to be like nothing. It is going to be as if I had never existed at all, and that never had anything else ever existed—it is just going to be as if I never was." And then I think, "Well, wasn't that just the way it was before I was born?" Thinking backwards in time, I can remember to a certain distance, and then I come to a total blank. And yet, here I am. I have emerged out of that total blank. And so have we all.

Have you ever tried to realize total blankness? I often think that the best way of doing that might be to try and look at my head with my own eyes. Because no matter how I turn around, I cannot see my own head. It isn't that there is a black spot behind my eyes, but that there is a total blank—the same kind of total blank, or nothingness, as that out of which I entered this world. At night I look at the stars, and I see them as vividly real, energetic points of fire scattered all over the sky in the middle of black nothingness. Now, how do you think the stars would look if there were no space? How would space look if there were no stars? You see, the two go together. You cannot realize what you mean by "is" unless you also have along with it a thing which you understand as "isn't." Void goes with form.

The Buddhist sutra says: "That which is form, that exactly is emptiness; that which is emptiness, that exactly is form." And all mysticism is comprised in this. Mysticism, as we use it in English, comes from the Greek word *muein*, which means, the finger on the lips, quiet, "mum's the word,"—we cannot really say it. You see, there is a secret. There is something that you are not supposed to know, but that you really should know for your sanity, and we are going to pass it on to you "on the q.t." In ancient times, it really was "on the q.t." but nowadays *nothing* is "on the q.t."—*everything* has been published. All knowledge is available, and there is no possibility anymore of there being anything esoteric. Everyone has smoked marijuana or taken LSD and practiced yoga, and so all this is simply a matter of public discussion. It is of the essence of scientific honesty to make all information public. And it is also the essence of democracy: if we are a republic, where all men are equal, then every single citizen of the United States, however well or not-well educated, has a right of access to *all* information.

That is supposedly what we believe in; which is another way of saying that you are all God. There is not someone else who is God, like some sort of boss over you, because that would be a monarchy and not a republic. But the trouble with the United States is that it is a republic peopled by those who believe that the universe is a monarchy. Therefore, they take an attitude which is paternalistic and authoritarian, and yet this is in direct conflict with the basic ideas upon which people like Thomas Jefferson and Benjamin Franklin founded this republic. This is the basic social conflict which we have to face; but let us go back to our more universal problem, called death.

We can see by a very simple process that when we die, we go into a negative dimension of consciousness, as we do when we sleep every night. Sleep is a very little understood phenomenon by psychologists, but what is obvious to us all is that sleep refreshes us. It is curious, but being unconscious for a while, being nowhere, brings us back to life. Of course it does! Because we wouldn't know we were alive unless we had once been dead, or unless we occasionally went to sleep. We wouldn't have the feeling of reality, of here-ness, of now-ness, of sensitivity, unless it could be contrasted with nowhere, or nothingness.

All knowledge, and all energy, is a phenomenon of contrasts. Like a wave. All energy is basically a wave phenomenon—there is the crest and the trough. It is at times upstanding, or convex, and at other times, down-standing, or concave. This is the difference between male and female. And if we understand this, we are not going to have anymore fights about women's lib. The male is upstanding, the female is hollow; and you cannot realize the one without the other. This is absolutely basic. You cannot see the figure without the ground, and you cannot understand what is important without what is unimportant. All logic, all discourse, all thought, all imagination, all consciousness, depends upon this contrast. And the secret of it is that the two go together. And this is what I was talking about as "mum's the word," *muein*—that what appears to be things opposed, unrelated, fighting (as in the various religions of the world), are really things that cannot do without each other.

Just before he died in 1958, I was visiting Carl Jung at his summer house on the edge of Lake Zurich. We were walking alongside the lake, with swans swimming nearby, and at the end of our talk I said to him, "Is it true that swans are monogamous?" And he said, "Why yes, it is curious that they are monogamous. And do you know, another interesting fact about swans is that when the male and female begin to make love to each other they start by fighting until they discover what they are supposed to be doing." Then he said, "This has been of great help to some of my female homosexual patients;" but he didn't explain it any further, he just dropped it and left it at that.

So you see, "make love, not war," is a very great statement, not of an ideal, but of a necessity. It is something that we are going to have to do whether we like it or not, because the opposite, the things that we seem to see as in absolute conflict—consciousness and un-consciousness, life and death, black and white—are absolutely essential to each other. And we can suddenly flip this into any dimension of human experience.

Let us take black people and white people—which is purely a caricature, because there really aren't black people and white people, there are brown people and greyish-pink people—but nevertheless, we'll call them black and white. And what I hope you see by this is that we can only realize the richness of experience because there is this differentiation. For instance, the way black people swing and behave wouldn't be recognizable unless it were in contrast with the way white people behave. The two groups should learn to be thankful to each other for their differences. So too, with man and woman, *Vive la petite difference!*. Long live the difference!

I might also express my point by asking you to consider all in-groups. Those people who see themselves as elect and saved, like the church, must realize that they can only understand themselves in contrast to an out-group—those who are the damned, all those awful people who live on the other side of the tracks, or in hell. Even St. Thomas Aquinas gave away the secret when he said that the saints in heaven occasionally walk to the edge of the battlements and look down at the squirming, burning, sufferings of the damned in hell and give praise to God for the administration of divine justice. He said that! In this way, the saints, by contrast with the sufferings of the damned, know in what bliss they are.

Now, I hope you realize that I am sort of making jokes and giving parables to express the point that we only know what reality is, or what it is to be alive and to exist, by contrast with nothingness, space, emptiness, and death. The one generates the other. and you might also understand this by considering the word "clarity." What do you think of when you say "clear"? Well, you might think of clear in the sense of wiped clean, transparent, or empty space; or as a finely polished mirror, or perfect, flawless lens. But the next thing you think of as clear might be a completely articulate form—something with outlines that are perfectly definite and totally in focus. Now, isn't it fascinating that in the idea of clarity, we have both emptiness and form in perfect expression? This is the meaning of the Buddhist saying which I referred to earlier: "emptiness is form, form is emptiness"—all is embraced in the idea of clarity.

Another fundamental contrast in our experience, like form and space, is the voluntary and the involuntary—what you do on the one hand, and what happens to you on the other. This is absolutely basic to most of us. We know, or we think we know, that there is a thing called "what I am doing" along with my influence on it, while on the other hand there is its influence on me—self and other. And our big struggle is to make "self" win over "other". This is what we call the conquest of nature. Collectively, humanity, as self, wants to subdue, beat down and control, what is called "other". But do we really want that? If we succeeded in that enterprise, that is, if we put the element of experience—the things that happen to us which are not in our control—in our complete control, we would be bored to death. It would be like screwing a plastic woman. Nobody wants that. When you love someone you want them to come at you in an unexpected, or spontaneous, way. You want to feel that there is something out there that is different, that will surprise you.

In exactly the same way, you would not be able to experience the situation that you call "self," as being a source of action more or less in control, unless it had the contrasting field of something "other" that is not in its control. Thus, you never know what that is going to be, and yet these two sensations go together, they are back and front of the same coin.

Following this line of reasoning, have you ever considered the possibility that the whole technological enterprise of the West, which is designed to control the universe by technological methods, is in the final analysis not sufficiently conscious of itself to know where it is going.

We do not comprehend our direction because it is not part of our education that we understand the relationship between opposites. We are so frantic to survive, and so terrified of night, and of death, that we are going to destroy the planet out of our anxiety to survive. The whole colossal military enterprise is wasting the energies of the earth in the most appalling way. The Americans, the Russians, and the Chinese are squandering their substance in the creating of so-called defensive technology—instruments intended to protect themselves from each other—which can only destroy us all. They can do nothing else. They protect no one. "Join the Air Force, and be safe"—you'll be the only ones who will be. Women and children can go hang; no one is going to protect them anymore. The whole technology of the military world is completely wasteful and destructive, and it is all being financed by *you* in the name of survival! In other words, you want to survive so badly that you are going to have to commit suicide.

So the point is: we do not *need* to survive. Let's get that into our heads! We don't really have to go on living, because the nothingness of death, being the opposite of life, simply generates it. The empty space of the sky is what is generating the stars, and the hollowness of the womb is what generates living beings. The emptiness is the form. But this is not in our logic, it was left out of our education. We never saw it, and therefore, we have anxiety all the time. We think: "To be or not to be, that is the question"—but it isn't. To be is not to be, and not to be is to be. They imply each other. They are the background. And so..., stop worrying!

Now, please understand, I am not saying all this just to be some kind of sophist, who enjoys throwing funny ideas at you. I am here to suggest that it is very important at this time in our evolution that we human beings cool it. That we reduce the volume of our anxiety and learn to take things easier. That we eat less, run around less, fuss less, and worry less about *being there*. I seriously do suggest this.

Now look, a lot of people do not know they are alive unless they are making a tremendous vibration. A lot of people need to get behind the wheel of a car or plane that goes vvvrrooooomm! And then they really know they are there: "Oh my, I'm a man!" And this is fouling the atmosphere, and creating an immense noise—it is making a great impression. Yes, but seriously, do you really have to? Do you have to expend all that energy to realize you are there? Are you like some people who always have to get into a fight, who've got to hit someone to know that "I can knock you down, and that tells me that I'm real"? Is that really necessary?

I would like to suggest that you can just as equally well know that you are real by humming to yourself. Instead of making a colossal din or a spectacle of prize fighting, you can know reality, and its energy, by simply humming to yourself or with other people—you know, we could all have a mutual hum: *oommmmmmm, oommmmmmm, oommmmmmmm...* and you can dig that, you can get with it, you can get right into it. You can feel that soft, deep energy, and you won't have to go roaring around, knocking people over the head, and so on.

If you can just get with this, you'll see that this is the life thing going, this is God. And you can hold hands, and sit around in a circle, and go *oommmmmm, oommmmmmmm, oommmmmmmm.......* and I realize this sounds silly to Americans. They will say, "What will happen to progress if people do that?" Well, as G.K. Chesterton once said: "Progress is finding a good place to stop."

5

HISTORICAL BUDDHISM

Mahayana Buddhism was India's principal export to the civilization of Asia, and quite basically, it's an attitude to life, based on complete non-fear, or you could call it, "Not clinging to things." It's based on the realization that you are not just your organism, your physical body, or your own particularized psyche. But that you, even if you don't know it consciously, (just as you don't know consciously how to grow your hair), you are fundamental reality, which is beyond any limitation of time or space—you're It. You're what there is.

The Hindus have a symbol for this thing that they call the Brahmin, the Atman, the Self. The Buddhists simply modify this by saying if you have a symbol of it, which is something that you believe in, as one might say, believe in God, or believe in Heaven, or life after death, or in an immortal soul; the fact that you believe is still an act of attachment or clinging—which is unnecessary.

And so, an unnecessary thing is what we would call, "Gilding the lily," or they use a wonderful phrase in Zen Buddhism, "Putting legs on a snake." Now, legs embarass a snake—it needs no legs. And gilt kills the lily. So, the Buddhists have worked out a religion of no religion, that is to say, in not believing in anything at all—not because they believe that reality is nothingness, but because believing is unnecessary. It's gilding the lily. So, this was the fundamental idea of this morning's lecture.

Now, I want to go on this afternoon and put some of this in a kind of systemmatic and historical perspective, so that you all know where we are in time, and in space, and what this is all about, and how it came to be. Though the funny thing is that the Indians have no sense of history whatsoever. This is one of the fundamental gripes of Western scholars. That when they read all the documents of Indian literature, there is no historical consciousness running in it, and so, you don't know what period it comes from.

To begin with, they didn't start writing anything down until about two centuries B.C., maybe a little before. Prior to that, everything was transmitted orally, and nobody has the faintest idea how far back it goes. The average educated guess today is that the Upanishads go back to about 800 B.C., and they are poems which represent the standpoint of Vedanta. Vedanta means: *danta*—almost our word for end or completion, of *veda*.

Veda is our word video, *videre*—to see. Vid is knowledge. And so, the most ancient scriptures of India are called *veda*, or vision, you see. They are poems in a mythological form, and the Upanishads constitute *veda-anta*, that is to say, "The completion of the vision," and they tell you the secret—the inner meaning that underlies the mythology.

So, let us presume that the most educated guess of scholars today is that the text called the Vedas are about 1500 B.C., and the text called Upanishads run from approximately 800 to considerably later—800 to at least 100, and some even later than that. But the major Upanishads such as the Brihadaranyaka, the Kana, the Isha and the Mondioku Upanishad, all are relatively early, so they will be anywhere from 800 to 600, prior to the time of Buddha. But still, you see, we're very vague about when all this started, because the Vedic tradition was brought to India from somewhere in central Asia.

The Arians who constitute the castes, the ruling people of India (and have done so for hundreds and hundreds of years) came from somewhere to the north, and have common ancestry linguistically with our European languages, but they had no sense of history.

If you write a story about a certain king who was involved with a certain sage, you alter the name of the king every time you re-tell the story—you simply make him the king of the present time, because then it becomes relevant... so nobody knows. The Jews, on the other hand, had a sense of history, and were very particular about when, and where, and what happened. So, it's far easier to make clear dates about the Old Testament, and compare them with archeological remains, than it is with anything from India, especially. India is a tropical country where everything decays quickly. It is a kind of swarming, lively, slimy turnover of life, so no one can be sure when all this started. So, to even Buddhism being a relatively late phenomenon out of Indian culture, the dates are a little bit more certain than they are with Hinduism.

So, we know that Gautama, the Buddha, lived shortly after 600 B.C.—but we are very, very uncertain as to what he taught. There are two great sections of Buddhist scriptures: One is written in the Pali language, and the other in Sanskrit. Although most of the Sanskrit texts no longer exist, and have to be studied in either Tibetan or Chinese translations, Western scholars are largely of the opinion that the Pali books represent more definitely the authentic teaching of the Buddha than the Sanskrit ones. Although, there's room for debate on this still. Pali is a sort of colloquial, south Indian form of Sanskrit. For example, if you say "Nirvana" in Sanskrit, you say *Nibana* in Pali; if you say "Karma" in Sanskrit, you say *Kama* in Pali. It's softened. So, all southern Buddhists, Theravadens, Inayana, make the Pali text their authority. And the earliest Pali texts we have are written on strips of palm leaf like this, just about so long, with characters which look like they are almost indistinguishable from the figure eight, unless you look very closely.... And they have holes in the middle of the leaves so that they can be strung together, and set between two boards of wood.

Well, now when you look at this record of the Buddhist teaching, you raise questions, because no human being sitting around in conversation with other people could have ever spoken this way. It simply is not natural conversation. What it is, is a highly tabulated form of instruction, tabulated in order to be memorized, so that it is easy to remember things if you classify them under one, two, three, four, five, six, seven, eight, nine, ten. Buddhism is all numbers.

There are three characteristics of being: *Duca*—suffering, *Anitia*—impermanence, and *Atna*—no self. There are Four Steps. There are Four Noble Truths. There are Eight stages of the Noble Eightfold Path. There are Ten Fetas. There are Twelve Elements of the Chain of Dependent Origination. Everything is numbered. And this, therefore, takes us back to a time before writing, when everything had to be committed to memory.

Now, it is conceivable that if I were going to talk to you, and I were going to examine you later, to be sure that you understood everything I said, that I would number my remarks, and say, "Now, you've got to remember first this, second that, third that," and I would talk back to you, and say, "What was the first thing, what was the second thing, what was the third thing? But the style of those Pali scriptures is so artificial, and everything is repeated again, and again and again, so that it's, quite honestly, something that monks put together on a wet afternoon, with nothing better to do. It is terribly boring, and I simply don't advise anybody, (except a serious scholar who wants to comb it all out, and get the results) ever to bother reading the Pali scriptures.

The advantage of the Christians, you see, is they have this inimitably beautiful English bible, translated under the reign of King James, and it is so exquisitely done.... And the Jews were great poets, and it is very readable. Buddhist scriptures are boring to the extreme, with exceptions.

There is this body of Pali literature which is called *Tipitika*. Tipitika means, "Three baskets," because the palm leaf manuscripts were stored in baskets, and three big baskets constitute the tradition of Hinayana, or Therabada Buddhism. In addition to this, there is the Mahayana Canon, or body of scriptures, which is one of the single biggest bodies of literature in the world. It is somewhat larger than the Encyclopedia Brittanica, and the official edition, existing today, is called the Tishodizokio, which is the Japanesse edition of the Chinese texts; and the other is called the Tung-jur, which is the Tibetan edition—but that's not so easily come by. But the standard edition of the Tishodizokio is a great, vast collection of volumes, all in Chinese, translating the Sanskrit scriptures.

Now again, the general opinion of scholars is that the Mahayana sutras are from a later time than the Buddha, the important texts in this collection, range in origin from 100 B.C., approximately to about 400 A.D. And so, according to the standards of Western scholarship, these are forgeries. They are attributed to the Buddha, but were actually composed by individuals living a lot later.

Our morals, our literary morals, would say this is forgery, and that has a bad intent, but this is a modern idea. If we go back to Western scriptures, for example, you will see a book in the Apocrypha called the *Wisdom of Solomon*, *The Song of Songs*, attributed to Solomon, the book of *Proverbs* in the Old Testament, attributed to Solomon. It is absolutely inconceivable that Solomon wrote these books. The book of *Deuteronomy* is attributed to Moses. It is absolutely impossible that Moses wrote the book of Deuteronomy. But why is it attributed to Moses? Because the actual writer of this book was too modest to give it his own name, and he would therefore say, "I feel that I have been into a center of my consciousness that is beyond me, and I am reporting things from a level of my being which I cannot claim as my own. Therefore, I have to ascribe the authorship to a person who is archetypal."

Solomon represents wisdom, so certain Hebrew writers, at certain periods of history, when they felt that they were in touch with real wisdom, would feel it immoral to say, "I, Ishmael Ben Ezra, will put this forth in my own name. On the contrary, that would be very immodest. I say, this is a revelation from Solomon." In those days, before copyright it was considered the ethical thing to do.

So, in exactly the same way, Indian Buddhists, living long after the Buddha, living, say in the University of Malanda, around the beginning of the Christian era. No, Malanda is later than that, Malanda takes us to 200 A.D., specifically to a man called Nagajuna, who lived about 200 A.D., who was the blinking genius of the whole Mahayana movement (we don't know whether Nagajuna wrote the scriptures he commented on, or only wrote the commentaries). But there's a huge body of literature in Sanskrit, and is known to us mainly through it's Tibetan and Chinese translations, called Pragnaparamita. *Pragna*, as I explained to you, means "intuitive wisdom". *Paramita*—"a going across", that is to say, to the "other shore". Wisdom for crossing to the other shore.

Almost all of this literature has been translated into English by Edward Conzy, and you can get selections from it in his book, which is now available in paperback in the Harper Torch Book series, *Buddhist Texts Through the Ages*. For the average person who does not want to be a specialist scholar, but wants to get a good idea about what all this is about, this is it. It has excellent selections from all types of Buddhist literature, and especially this class.

It is conceivable that Nagajuna wrote the scriptures, in the name of the Buddha. And others did, too. But they were simply, by their standards, too modest to say, "This is mine." They are saying, "It comes from a deeper level of consciousness than my ego, and therefore is the Buddha's." Now, you see, in our morals, that's forgery. In their morals, it's not.

In Buddhism, you don't have the same problem that you have in Christianity. In Christianity, we want to know, what were the very words of Jesus? And what was a late edition? The authority is so peculiarly involved in the historical Jesus. In Buddhism this is not the case. The Buddhists, in general, feel that Buddhism is like a tree. Buddha planted the seed, and later the tree grows. Very definitely. You see, in Christianity, Jesus is the *only* incarnation of God. The Christian, orthodox Christians, will on the whole argue—there will never be, there was never, another incarnation of God.

But in Buddhism, it is of the essence of the thing that Buddhas can appear in the world again, and again and again. Anyone of you can become a Buddha. So there isn't this fastening of authority to a particular historical time and place. So then, the Buddhist scriptures represent, although they are all attributed to the Buddha, they represent an uncovering of questions which the Buddha raised.

For this purpose, it's important to understand one thing that is not made clear in almost all the books on Buddhism that I have ever read. Buddhism is absolutely, fundamentally a dialogue. And this dialogue, which is an interchange between a teacher and an inquirer, (as were the teachings of Socrates) is quite different from an authoritative pronouncement. There are no teachings of Buddhism. Everything you will find stated as a teaching of Buddhism, is actually a question, not a teaching.

Let's go to a very fundamental point. Buddhism deals with the problem of suffering. Because after all, suffering is the problem, that's what we mean by the whole idea of a problem. I suffer. I have a problem. So, if you don't like suffering, you say, "How do I not suffer?" And you go to a wise guy and say, "I am in pain. I'm anxious, I'm afraid, I'm this, that and the other. How do I not do it?" So the Buddha answers to this question, "You suffer because you desire. If you didn't desire, your desires would never be frustrated, and so you wouldn't suffer. So, what would happen if you didn't desire?"

This is not a teaching. It is not saying, "You ought not to desire." It is a request for making an experiment. Could you possibly not desire? So the inquirer goes away and he makes this experiment. He says, can I possibly get rid of my desires? And he discovers in the course of making this experiment that he is desiring to get rid of his desires. And so, he returns to the teacher, and says, "It is impossible not to desire, because in trying not to desire, I'm desiring." And the teacher says, "You're getting warmer." You see, in every respect, everything that the Buddha ever suggested that his followers should do, was by nature of an experiment. Buddhism never uttered it's final teaching. What it was actually after, all it describes are various experiments you can make to get on the road to it.

It is of the nature of it that it is a dialogue. Indeed, many of the books of the Pali scriptures are called

Dialogues of the Buddha. This is very, very important to understand—that all these records and scriptures are interchanges.

One of the first things, for example, when I was starting to study Buddhism in my teens, was that I met a wonderful Japanese Sanskrit professor, and he explained to me: "Buddha taught three kinds of being: *Duca*—the world as we live it is suffering, *Amitia*—impermanent, and *Atman*—without self." And he said, "Buddha teach duca, to contradict wrong view, duca. Buddha teach amitia, contradict wrong view amitia."

This is wonderful. The whole idea, you see is, you don't, you can't say what the truth is. So there is no dogma. All you do is, you get going a dialogue, the effect of which is to counterbalance people's wrong view, or partial view. All Buddhism is view, the way you look at it. See?

So, the first step of the Noble Eightfold Path is called, *Samyadrishti*, which means: *Sumya*—perfect, our word sum, summation, it comes eventually from the Sanskrit, *samyag*, meaning perfect view.

There's a wonderful story about Suzuki, who was giving a course on Buddhism at the University of Hawaii, and he was going through the Four Noble Truths, and he got to the fourth one, and he was lazing around on a hot afternoon with a group of students, half-asleep, as he is often as an old man, and he said, "First step of Noble Eightfold Path is *Sho-ken*, mean right view, complete view. All Buddhism is view. You have right view, you have all Buddhism. Right view is no special view. Second step of Noble Eightfold Path... I forget second step. You look it up in the book." So, I told this story to Sabro Hasegawa of Kioto, and he said, "First step of Noble Eightfold Path, in Japanese, *sho-kien, sho* means correct, *kien* means view, he said is *ssh.*"

What you have to understand then, simply, is that you can't look up the teachings of Buddhism in the same way that you can look up the teachings of Hegel, Kant, Spinoza, Jesus Christ, Thomas Aquinas, Aristotle, and so on. They don't exist—they've never been written down. All that has been written down is the dialogue that leads up to the understanding.

Somebody raised the question in this morning's discussion about whether you needed other people. Was it you, Virginia? And in a way you do, because this is the need of the guru. Now the guru is not necessarily somebody who is a qualified master. The guru is something against which you bounce. It may be a book. It may be your own reflection in the mirror, said I to myself, said I?

But this dialogue is *the way* in Buddhism. Question. Answer. That's why all those Zen stories are *mondo* which means question-answer. The whole body of literature is simply a feeling out of a question. So then, what's the question? "What's going on?" As I said, the basic question, the way Buddhism approaches it is: "I suffer, what shall I do about it?" Answer: "You suffer because you desire, try not to desire." Next question:

"But I'm desiring not to desire." Next answer: "Try not even to desire not to desire."

Or, put it in this way—don't desire not to desire any more than you can manage. In other words, accept the facts as they are. But then, I find I can't help desiring to a certain extent that always makes me uncomfortable. Well, the question comes back, "Who is it that's uncomfortable? Who's complaining? Who are you?"

This is always what it gets down to. Who raises the question? Who, in other words, is in conflict with the universe? Find out who *you* are, and this is always peculiarly difficult, because it's like trying to look at your own eyes without using a mirror, or to bite your own teeth—to define yourself.

And so, all this literature is really the gyrations of somebody trying to find who he is, which will never succeed. And that is why it's called the Doctrine of the Void. That one really has to be reconciled, not only reconciled to, but delighted with—the fact that you, yourself, are basically indefinable. If you *were* definable, you would be a mortal thing like anything else. And you would just dissolve. But so long as you're *not* definable, you're eternal. As much of you as you *can't* catch hold of, is the *real* you. But the price you pay for this, the privilege of being eternal, is that you don't know it. You can't grab onto it! See?

This comes out of sorrows. In the Buddhism that we have in the Pali Canon, the dialogue goes as far as all the techniques for renouncing desire, so that the general trend of Saravata Buddhism is ascetic. But what happened historically was, that many of those monks who practiced all the ascetic exercises, started to ask themselves the question, "Why are we doing this?" And they discovered that the reason they were practicing the ascetic exercises was that they were scared of life, and wanted to get out of it, which nullifies the effect of those exercises. In other words, they were acting in an unselfish way, for selfish reasons. And all those monks who were simply naive and perceptive enough to recognize this, then moved on into the Mahayana stage of development.

You can go through a tough meditation discipline where you try to control your thoughts completely, and not think anything lustful, or harmful, or selfish, and so on, but you are eventually compelled to come to the question, "Why are you doing this?" And the answer is, of course, the same old reason I started with. "I desire." And this is still desire. So, then the dialogue has to be carried on from that point, in such a way, that the problem is increasingly thrown back at the source of the question. "Who's asking? Why asking?" Until, you see what they call in Zen that you are raising waves when no wind is blowing. You are making the problem.

And this comes back, you see, to the most fundamental, original ideas of Buddhism, which Sir Edwin Arnold expresses in his poem about the teaching of the Buddha, "Ye suffer from yourselves, None else compels, None other holds you that you live and die,

And whir upon the wheel, And hug and kiss its spokes of agony, its tire of tears, its nave of nothingness."

But, you see, the whole game we play with ourselves is, "I'm not responsible." A person can turn back to their parents, and say, "You got me in this mess. You two males and females were having fun in bed together, and as a result of this, you irresponsibly created me. And you didn't provide for me properly. You were economically unsound or something, and I blame you for all this." See? What an alibi that is, and all life is based on this game. And nobody will admit, you see, that the evil gleam in your father's eye when he was after your mother, was *you!* That same surge of life was just the same as you are. See?

You started the problem. And you can't just blame somebody else, because if you blame your parents, and they are in any way blameworthy, they can always blame *their* parents, for getting them in the mess, and on it goes way back to Adam and Eve. And you know what happened then? When the trouble started, God came around and said to Adam, "Man, what have you done?" And he said, "This woman that Thou gavest, she tempted me, and I did eat." And then God went and looked at Eve. And she said, "The serpent gave it to me." And then God looked at the serpent, and the serpent didn't say anything, because the serpent knew all too well what the story was, but wasn't gonna let on.

You see, because the serpent is the unacknowledged part of God, only it mustn't be. Let not your left hand know what your right hand doeth. Especially let not your right hand know what your left hand doeth because the right hand is the hand that's honest. Shake hands with the right hand, eat with the right hand. But the left hand is the inauspicious hand. With that you clean up messes, and you eat with the other see, so you don't get the two mixed. Mustn't get your head mixed up with your tail. So this is called the Seen Hand, and this is the Obscene Hand. This is inpropitious, this is propitious, unpropitious, propitious. So, keep that going see, don't let go, don't give away the secret of these two hands, or that the two ends are all one.

In Mythology, the serpent Ouroborus is eating it's own tail. Now this actually means it's nourishing itself on its own excrement. But it doesn't know it. If it did know it, it wouldn't. So there is, just behind the serpent's head an unconscious place. You see, your eyes look out this way, they don't look back that way, and by virtue of that, you make a block of unconsciousness in the circle, so that you don't know what you're getting is what comes from you. And so long as you don't know, you keep it up.

If you say, "Well I, after all, realize this is nothing but me." And they say, "Well, why bother? It's just going round and around." And that's why total omnipotence or omniscience would have no future in it—because you could do nothing, you could know nothing except what you already know, and you'd know all of that. There would be no surprises. And the moment there isn't a surprise, that means there isn't something unconscious, then you won't have any life. So it all depends that anything happens at all, on there being, besides being, besides power, besides consciousness, besides pleasure, non-being, impotence, unknowing, pain. Without this *nothing* happens.

So then, if you say, "Oh, but I want to get rid of that side of things which is non-being, unknowing, impotence, pain"—the teacher is trying to show you by the dialogue that you don't understand the way you have stated your own question. You haven't thought it through. You are, in other words, desiring something that you don't want.

Let's suppose a very simple illustration of this. I don't want to die. O.K! You have the problem of the Wandering Jew, who cannot die, who's condemned to life, so that when he throws himself into the ocean, it throws him out. He casts himself into the fire, and the fire shrivels. You *cannot* die. And you realize what a horror this state is, because you can't forget. You must go on accumulating memories forever, and ever, and ever, and ever, until you become sick, you get indigestion with the multiplicity of memories. But people don't ordinarily think this through. They say, "I'd like to go on living always, please, I don't want to die, not yet, no." For they don't think it through. They say, "I want to go to Heaven. I want to be reunited with all my friends and relations, and be happy forever, and ever, and ever."

They don't realize what an absolute *bore* this state could be! You would be horrified if you don't think it through. The point of the dialogue is that the teacher forces you to think through all your desires. Be careful of what you desire, you may get it!

And you know, this is the story about the three wishes. There was, once upon a time, a person who discovered the ear of the statue of the Oracle, Adelphi, in Greece. It was found in an antique shop, wrapped in a little sliver of paper which said, "Be back by 3".

This came into the hands of two very intelligent gentlemen. (I'm repeating a story that Gerald Hurd told) These very intelligent gentlemen had a dinner party one evening in the presence of this ear, and they discussed what it meant. They said, "Look, this ear is probably a wishing ear, you whisper things into it. Let's try and work it out."

So, you know how people are when they get in the presence of magic, they always ask it to do something trivial—they said, "Make this vase turn upside-down. This is our first wish." How stupid can you get, you know? So, they did that.

Well, apparently nothing happened. But in a little while they all began to feel funny, and they felt more comfortable with their arms up in the air, than lying on the table. What had happened was, indeed, their gravity was reversed from the gravity of the vase. And they were very uncomfortable about this. So, with what did they have now? Two wishes left. (There are always three wishes.)

What was the second wish? Obviously to undo the first. So they said, "Let everything be as it was before we wished." And they were comfortable again.

Now they had but one wish left, with no possibility of reverting it. And one of the men said, "Let's not take it, let's just abandon the whole thing." But the other was an adventurous man, and he grabbed the ear and said, "I wish not to wish".

At that moment, the stone ear leapt out of his hand and fell on the hearth, and hissed in flame, and dissolved. But suddenly they found themselves sitting there in peace. Everything was just right the way it was, because they had wished not to wish.

So, to desire not to desire must finally include the fact you see, that you do desire. And that this is a feature of your nature, in just the same way as blue is a feature of the sky, that feet have five toes each on them. You desire, and if you desire not to desire, that is to say you desire not to be a human being, you're fighting the facts, which as a matter of fact, are your own facts.

The whole secret of the matter is that we construct our psychology so that we experience a whole segment of our experience as something that's put on us. It's the same thing as you blame your parents by saying, "You brought me into this world", or "Water is wet, fire is hot, and I did not bargain for this, I didn't arrange it." So by having a whole segment of our experience that we don't assume responsibility for, and we say, "*You* did it!" Then it's not my fault! You see, this is, it is *this* that creates the problem.

Q. May I interject a question?

A. Yes.

Q. How do you explain the Buddhist monk's vow of um, to free himself from desire? Isn't that one of the vows?

A. Yes of course. Where he says in the Mahayana Vows, "However innumerable the hang-ups are, I vow to conquer them all." *Kesha* in Sanskrit, the hang-ups.

Q. How do I vow to keep myself from the passions.

A. Yes, they're the Kesha. Yes.

Q. But yet, a true Mahayana Buddhist would assume that you are the passions. You could not be you without these passions.

A. Right, right.

Q. So how can you free yourself?

A. So, you set your self the infinite task.

Q. I've been perplexed by that. Could it possibly be that the, could the keyword be that you won't be deluded by the whole problem of passion?

A. See again, that the vows must be understood in the context of the dialogue. Undertaking these vows is part of being involved in a dialogue with a teacher, and the teacher suggests that you undertake these vows—which are ridiculous.

Q. *Well, that's my objection!*

A. Sure, but you won't find out that they're ridiculous unless you try them.

Q. *But, they're magical, in a certain sense—I'm speaking personally.*

A. Oh, sure they are! Well, look, we're going to have an intermission.

6

PHILOSOPHY
OF NATURE

I want to talk to you a bit about the general purpose of this tour. I might say that I'm interested in Japanese materialism, because contrary to popular belief, Americans are not materialists. We are not people who love material, but our culture is by and large, devoted to the transformation of material into junk, as rapidly as possible. God's own junkyard! And therefore it's a very, very important lesson for a wealthy nation, and for a rich people. And we are all colossally rich by the standards of the rest of the world. It's very important for such people to learn and see what happens to material in the hands of people who love it.

And so, you might say that in Japan, and in China, but in Japan in a peculiar way, the underlying philosophy of life is a spiritual materialism. There is not the divorce between soul and body, between spirit and matter, between spirit and nature, or God and nature, which there is in the West. And therefore, there is not the same kind of contempt for material things. We regard matter as something that gets in our way, something whose limitations are to be abolished as fast as possible, and therefore we have bulldozers and every kind of technical device for knocking it out of the way. And we like to do as much obliteration of time and space as possible. We talk about killing time, and getting there as fast as possible, but of course, as you notice in Tokyo, and as your noticing here, the nearer it gets to you by time, by the abolition of distance, the more it's the same place from which you started.

This is one of the great difficulties—what is going to happen to this city, and this country when it becomes the same place as California. In the same way, in other words, you could take a streetcar from one end of town to another, and it's the same town. So, if you can take a jet plane from one city to another (and everybody's doing it, not just the privileged few), then they're going to be the same town.

So, to preserve the whole world from indefinite Los Angelization, pardon me, those of you from Southern California, but, we have to learn in the United States, how to enjoy material, and to be true materialists, instead of exploiters of material. And so, this is the main reason for going into philosophy of the Far East, and how it relates to every day life—to architecture, to gardens, to clothes, and to the higher arts of painting, tea ceremony, music, sculpture, ritual, and so on.

Well now, basic to all this is the philosophy of nature. And the Japanese philosophy of nature is probably founded historically in the Chinese philosophy of nature, and that's what I want to go into to start with. To let the cat out of the bag, right at the beginning, the assumptions underlying Far Eastern culture, (and this is true as far west as India, also) is that the whole cosmos, the whole universe, is one being.

It is not a collection of many different beings, who somehow floated together like alot of flotsam and jetsam from the ends of space, and ended up as a thing called the universe. They look at the world as one, eternal activity, and that's the only real self that you have. You are *theworks*—only what we call *you*, as a distinct organism, is simply a manifestation of the whole thing. Just as the ocean when it waves, it's the whole ocean waving when it waves. And the whole ocean, when it waves, it says, "*Yoo*-*Hoo*, I'm here!", you see. So each one of us is a wave of all that there is, of the whole works. And they don't, you see this is, in this culture, not something that is just a theory—not just an idea, like you would have, I have my ideas, you have your ideas, in other words, you're a Christian Scientist, I'm a Baptist, or something like that. No, or I'm a Republican, and you're a Democrat, and I'm a Bircher, and you're a communist. It isn't that kind of thing—it's not an opinion, it's a feeling.

And so, the great, the great men of this culture (not everybody), but the great men, the great masters, of whatever sphere they're in, are fundamentally of this feeling that what you are is the thing that always was, is and will be, only it's playing the game called, "Mr. Tocano," or "Mr. Lee," or "Mr. Mukapadya." That's a special game it's playing, just like there's the fish game, the grass game, the bamboo game, the pine tree game, they're all ways of going "Hoochie-koochie-doochie-doochie-doochie-doo." You see everything's doing a dance, only it's doing it according to the nature of the dance. The universe is fundamentally all these dances, whether human, fish, bird, cloud, sky dance, star dance, etc., they are all one fundamental dance. Or dancer. Only in Chinese, you don't distinguish the subject from the verb, I mean, you don't distinguish the noun from the verb in the same way that we do. A noun can become a verb, a verb can become a noun. But, that's the business.

A civilized, cultured, above all, an enlightened person, in this culture, is one who knows that his so-called "separate personality," his ego, is an illusion. Illusion doesn't mean a bad thing, it just means a play, from the Latin word, *ludere*, we get English illusion. Ludere means to play. So, the Sanskrit word, *maya*, meaning illusion, also means magic, skill, art, and this Sanskrit conception comes through China to Japan with the transmission of Buddhism.

The world as a *Maya*, or sometimes as it's called in Sanskrit: *lila*, (our word 'lilt'); Lila, is play. So, all individual manifestations are games, dances, symphonies, musical forms, being put on by the whole show. And everyone is basically the whole show, so that's the fundamental feeling.

But Nature, *Nature* as the word is used in the Far East doesn't mean quite the same as the word Nature in the West. In Chinese, nature, the word we translate nature, *zitran*, or in Japanese, *shizen*, is made up of two characters. That first one means "of itself," and the second one means "so". What is so, of itself. This is a rather difficult word to translate well into English. We might _say, automatic," but automatic suggests something mechanical.

When a Chinese coolie was supposed to have seen a tram car for the first time, he said, "No pushee, no pulley, go like mad!" But, uh, this mechanical idea of the automatic won't properly translate this word *zitran*, in Chinese, *shizen* in Japanese. Of itself so, what happens, or as we say, what comes naturally. It's in that sense of our word nature, to be natural, to act in accordance with one's nature, not to strive for things, not to force things, that they use the word natural. So, when your hair grows, it grows without your telling it to, and you don't have to force it to grow. So, in the same way, when the color of your eyes, whether it's blue or brown, or whatever, the eyes color themselves, and you don't tell them how to do it. When your bones grow a certain way, they do it all of themselves.

And so, in the same way, I remember a Zen master once, he was a beautiful man, he used to teach in New York. His name was Mr. Sazaki. One evening, he was sitting in his golden robes, in a very formal throne-like chair, with a fan in his hand, he had one of those fly-whisks made of a white horse's tail. And he was looking very, very dignified—incense burning on the table in front of him, there was a little desk with one of the scriptures on it that he was explaining. And he said, "All nature has no purpose. Purposelessness most fundamental principle of Buddhism, purposelessness. Ahhh, when you drop fart, you don't say, 'At nine o'clock I dropped fart,' it just happen.' "

So then, it's fundamental to this idea of nature, that the world has no boss. In, this is very important, especially if you're going to understand Shinto. Because, we translate, *kami*, or *shin* as God, but it's not God in that sense. God, in much of the Western meaning of the word, means "the controller," "the boss of the world." And the model that we use for nature tends to be the model of the carpenter, or the potter, or the king. That, just as the carpenter takes wood and makes a table out of it, or as the potter takes inert clay, and with the intelligence of his hands evokes a form in it, or as the king is the law-giver who, from above, tells people what order they shall move in, and how they shall behave, it is ingrained into the Western mind to think that the universe is a behavior which is responding to somebody in charge, and understands it all.

When I was a little boy, and I used to ask my mother many questions, sometimes she'd get fed up with me, and say, "My dear, there are some things in this life that we are not just meant to know." And so I said, "Well, what about it? Will we ever know?" "Well," she said, "yes, when you die, and you go to Heaven, God will make it all clear."

And I used to think, that maybe, on wet afternoons in Heaven, we'd all sit around God's throne and say, "Heavenly Father, why are the leaves green?" And he would say, "Because of the chlorophyll!" And we would say, "Oh!".

Well, that idea, you see, of the world as an artifact could prompt a child in our culture to say to it's mother, "How was I made?" And it seems very natural. So when it's explained that God made you, the child naturally goes on and says, "But who made God?" But, I don't think a Chinese child would ask that question at all, "How was I made?" Because the Chinese mind does not look at the world of nature as something manufactured, but rather grown.

The character for coming into being in Chinese is based on a symbol of a growing plant. Now growing and making are two different things. When you make something, you assemble parts, or you take a piece of wood and you carve it, working gradually from the outside inwards, cutting away until you've got the shape you want. But when you watch something grow, it isn't going like that.

If you see, for example, a fast motion movie of a rose growing, you will see that the process goes from the inside to the outside—it is, as it were, something expanding from the center. And that, so far from being an addition of parts, it all grows together, all moves all over itself at once. And the same is true when you're watching the formation of crystals, or even if you're watching a photographic plate being developed. Suddenly, all over the area of the plate, over the field, shall we call it, like a magnetic field, it all arises.

That idea of the world as growing, and as not obeying any laws, because there is in Chinese philosophy no difference between the Tao (that is the word t-a-o), the Japanese *do*, there is—no difference between the Way, the power of Nature, and the things in Nature.

It isn't, you see, when I stir up wind with this fan, it isn't simply that the wind obeys the fan. There wouldn't be a fan in my hand unless there were wind around. Unless there were air, no fan. So the air brings the fan into being as much as the fan brings the air into being. So, they don't think in this way of obeying all the time—masters and slaves, lord and servant.

Lao-Tse, who is supposed to have written the *Tao Te Ching*, the fundamental book of the Taoist philosophy, lived probably, a little before 300 B.C. Although tradition makes him a contemporary of Confucius, who lived closer to 600, he says in his book, "The great Tao flows everywhere, to the left and to the right. It loves and nourishes all things, but does not lord it over them. And when merits are attained, it makes no claim to them."

The corollary of that is, that if this is the way nature is run, not by government, but by, as it were, letting everything follow its course, then the skillful man or woman, or the skillful ruler, or the sage interferes as little as possible with the course of things. Of course you can't help interfering. Every time you look at something, you change it. Your existence is, in a way, an interference, but if you think of yourself as something separate from the rest of the world, then you will think of interference or not-interference. But if you know that you're not separate from it, that you are just as much in and of nature as the wind or the clouds, then who interferes with them?

In general, the notion is that life is most skillfully lived when one sails a boat, rather than rowing it. You see it's more intelligent to sail than to row. With oars I have to use my muscles and my effort to drag myself along the water, but with a sail, I let the wind do the work for me. More skillful still, when I learn to tack, and let the wind blow me against the direction of the wind. Now, that's the whole philosophy of the Tao. It's called in Chinese, *wu-wei*, *wu-non*, *wei*—striving. *Mui* is Japanese at pronouncing the Chinese *wei*. *Mu* is Chinese *wu*. *Mui*, as distinct from *ui*. *Ui* means to use effort—to go against the grain, to force things. *Mui*—not to go against the grain, to go with the grain.

And so, you will see around you, in every direction, examples of mui—of the intelligent handling of nature, so as to go with it rather than against it. For example, the famous art of Judo is entirely based on this. When you are attacked, don't simply oppose the force used against you, but go in the same direction as it's going, and lead it to its own downfall.

So it is said, in the winter, there's a tough pine tree, which has a branch like this, and muscles. And the snow piles up and piles up, and this unyielding branch eventually has this huge weight of snow, and it cracks. Whereas the willow tree has a springy, supple branch, and a little snow comes on it, and the branch just goes down, and the snow falls off, and whoops, the branch goes up again.

Lao-Tse said, "Man, at his birth is supple and tender, but in death, he is rigid and hard. Plants when they are young, are soft and supple, but in death they are brittle and hard. So, suppleness and tenderness are the characteristics of life, and rigidity and hardness the characteristics of death." He made many references to water. He said, "Of all things in the world, nothing is more soft than water, and yet it wears away the hardest rocks. Furthermore, water is humble, it always seeks the low level, which men abhor. But yet, water finally overcomes everything."

When you watch water take the line of least
resistance, you watch for example, water poured out on
the ground, then you see it, as it were, ejecting fingers
from itself, and some of those fingers stop. But, one
finger goes on—it's found the lowest level. Now, you say,
"Oh, but that's not the water, the water didn't do
anything, that's just the contours of the land, and because
of the contours of the land, the water goes where the land
makes it go." Think again.

Does the sailing boat go where the wind makes it go?
I never forget once, I was out in the countryside, and a
piece of thistle-down flew out of the blue. It came right
down near me, and I put out a finger, and I caught it by
one of its little tendrils. And it behaved just like catching
a daddy long-legs, you know, when you catch one by one
leg it naturally struggles to get away. Well, this thing
behaved just like that, and I thought well, "It was just the
wind doing that, it only appears to look as if it was doing
it." Then I thought again, "Wait a minute! It is the wind,
yes, but, it's also that this has the intelligence to grow
itself, so as to use the wind." You see that? That is
intelligence. That little structure of thistle-down is a form
of intelligence, just as surely, as the construction of a
house is a manifestation of intelligence. But it uses the
wind.

In the same way, the water uses the conformations
of the ground. Water isn't just dead stuff. It's not just
being pushed around. Nothing is being pushed around in
the Chinese view of nature. Because you see, my first

point as I've been saying, is what they mean by nature; that it is something that happens of itself—that it has no boss. The second point is that it does not. In the sense that it doesn't have a boss, somebody giving orders, somebody obeying orders, that leads further to an entirely different conception of cause and effect. Cause and effect is based on giving orders. When you say, "Something made this happen." It *had* to happen because of what happened before. The Chinese don't think like that. His idea of causality is called, or the concept which does duty for our idea of causality is called "mutual arsing."

Let's take the relationship between the back and the front of anything. Is the back the cause of the front, or is the front the cause of the back? What a silly question! If things don't have fronts, then they can't have backs. If they don't have backs, they can't have fronts. Front and back always go together, that is to say, they come into being together. And so, in just the same way as the front and the back arise together, the basic sort of Chinese Taoist philosophy sees everything in the world coming together.

This is called the Philosophy of Mutual Inter-penetration. In Japanese, *gi-gi-muge*. We'll go into this in detail when we get to *nara*, because *nara* is the center of Kegon Buddhism, and so, this is the particular philosophy which developed gi-gi-muge. But still, it goes way back into the history of the Chinese idea of nature.

Now look at it very simply. Let us suppose that you had never seen a cat, and one day you were looking through a very narrow slit in a fence, and a cat walks by. First you see the cat's head, then there's a rather non-descript fuzzy interval, and a tail follows. And you say, "Marvelous!" Then the cat turns 'round and walks back. You see the head, and then after a little interval, the tail. You say, "Incredible!" The cat turns around and walks back again, and you see first the head, and then the tail, and you say, "This begins to look like a regularity, there must be some order in this phenomenon, because whenever I see the thing which I've labelled head, I later see the thing I've labelled tail."

Therefore, where there is an event which I call head, and it's invariably followed by another event that I call tail, obviously head is the cause of tail, and the tail is the effect. Now, we think that way about everything. But of course, if you suddenly widened up the crack in the fence, so that you saw that the head and the tail were all one cat, and that the head, and when a cat is born, it's born with a head and a tail, it isn't that there is a head, and then later, a tail.

So, in exactly the same way, the events that we seem to call, "separate events," are really all one event, only we chop it into pieces to describe it. Like we say, "The head of the cat, and the tail of the cat," although it's all one cat. When we've chopped it to pieces, then we suddenly forget we did that, and try to explain how they fit together—and we invent a myth called "causality" to explain how they do. The reason we chop the world into bits is simply for purposes of intellectual convenience.

For example, our world is through and through wiggly, and you notice that very much, how these people, although they have models, symmetry and use of space in the construction of houses, they love wigglings and their garden, you see, is very fundamentally wiggly. They appreciate wiggly rocks. I remember so much as a child, wondering why Chinese houses all had wiggly roofs, the way they were curved. And why the people looked more wiggly than our people look. Cause the world is wiggly! Now, what are you gonna do with a wiggly world? You've gotta straighten it out! So we notice that the initial solution is to try and straighten it out.

People, of course, are very wiggly indeed. Only because we all appear together, do we look regular. You know, we have two eyes, one nose, one mouth, and two ears, and so on... We look regular so we make sense. But if somebody had never seen a person before, they'd say, "What's this extraordinary, amazing, wiggly phenomenon?" We are—the world is—*wiggly*.

One of the wiggliest things in the world is a fish. Somebody once found out they could use a net and catch a fish. Then they thought out a much better idea than that—they could catch the world with a net. A wiggly world. But what happens? Hang up a net in front of the world and look through it. What happens? You can count the wiggles, by saying, this wiggle goes so many holes across, so many holes down, so many holes across, so many to the left, so many to the right, so many up, so many down... What do you have? You have the genesis of the calculus. And your net, as it were, breaks up the world into countable bits, as we now say in information theory, "We have so many bits of information to process."

In the same way, a bit is a bite. You go to eat chicken, you can't swallow the whole chicken at once, so you've got to take it in bites. But you don't get a cut up fryer out of the egg. So in the same way the real universe has no bits. It's all one thing, it's not alot of things. In order to digest it with your mind, which thinks of one thing at a time, you've got to make a calculus, you've got to chop the universe into bits, so as to think about it, and talk about it.

You can see this whole fan at once, but if you want to talk about it, you have to talk about it bit by bit. Describe it, go into the details. What details? Well, so with the world. If you don't realize that's what you've done, that you've 'bitted' the world in order to think about it, it isn't really bitted at all. If you don't realize that, then you have troubles, because then you've got to explain how the bits go together. How they connect with each other— so you invent all sorts of ghosts, called "Cause and Effect", and influences. The word *influence*, you know— How do I influence *you?* As if I was something different from you. So influences, and ghosts and spooks, all these things come into being if we forget that we made the initial step of breaking the unity into pieces in order to discuss it.

So then, stepping back again, we have these very, very basic principles then. The world as nature, what happens of itself, is looked upon as a living organism, and it doesn't have a boss because things are not behaving in response to something that pushes them around. They are just behaving. And it's all one, big behavior. Only if you want to look at it from certain points of view, you can see it as if something else were making something happen. But you do that only because you divide the thing up.

"So now," you say, "final question. Is their nature chaotic? Is there no law around here?" There is not one single Chinese word that means the Law of Nature, as we use it. The only word in Chinese that means law as we use it is a word *tse*, and this word is a character which represents a cauldron with a knife beside it. And this goes back to the fact that in very ancient times, when a certain emperor made laws for the people, he had the laws etched on the sacrificial cauldrons, so that when the people brought the sacrifices they would read what was written on the cauldrons. And so this word, *tse*. But the sages, who were of a Taoist feeling at the time that this emperor lived said, "You shouldn't have done that, sir. Because the moment the people know what the law is, they develop a little dis-spirit. And they'll say, 'Well now, did you mean this precisely, did you mean that precisely. And we'll find a way of wrangling around it.' " So they said that the nature of nature, Tao, is *wut-se*, which means lawless, but in that sense of law.

But to say that nature is lawless is not to say that it's chaotic. Now the Chinese word here for the order of nature is called in Japanese *ri*, Chinese *li*. Ri, is a curious word, it originally meant "the markings in jade, the grain in wood, or the fibre in muscle." Now when you look at jade, you see it has this wonderful, mottled markings in it. And you know, somehow and you can't explain why, those mottlings are not chaotic. When you look at the patterns of clouds, or the patterns of foam on the water, isn't it astounding, they never, never make an aesthetic mistake.

Look at the way the stars are arranged, or they're *not* arranged! They're just like, they seem to be scattered through the sky like spray. But would you ever criticize the stars for being in poor taste? When you look at a mountain range—it's perfect. But somehow, this spontaneous, wiggly arrangement of nature is quite different from anything we would call a mess.

Look at an ashtray, full of cigarette butts and screwed bits of paper. Look at some modern painting, where people have gone out of their way to create the expensive messes. You see, they're different. And this is the joke, that we can't put our finger on what the difference is, although we jolly well know it. We can't define it. If we could define it... in other words, if we could define aesthetic beauty, it would cease to be interesting. In other words, if we could have a method that would automatically produce great artists, anybody could go to school and become a great artist. Their work would be the most boring kind of kittsch. But just because you don't know how it's done, that gives it an excitement.

And so it is with this. There is no formula, that is to say, no *tse*—no rule according to which all this happens. And yet it's not a mess. So this idea of *ri*, (you can translate the word *ri* as organic pattern). And this *ri* is the word that they use for the order of nature, instead of our idea of law, where the things are obeying something. If they are not obeying a governor, in the sense of God, they are obeying principles, like a streetcar. Do you know that limerick?

There was a young man who said, "Damn!"
For it certainly seems that I am
A creature that moves, in determinate grooves
I'm not even a bus, I'm a tram!

So that idea of the iron rails, along which the course of life goes is absent here. And that is why basically, this accounts for Chinese and Japanese humanism. And here (this is very important), there's a basic humanism to this culture. The people in this culture, Chinese and Japanese don't feel guilty ever. They feel ashamed, yes.. of something. Ashamed because they have transgressed social requirements. But they are incapable of a sense of

"Sin". They don't feel, in other words that you are guilty because you exist, you owe your existence to the Lord God, and you were a mistake anyway! You know? They don't feel that. They have social shame, but not metaphysical guilt, and that leads to a great relaxation. And you can sense it if you're sensitive, just walking around the streets. You realize that these people have not been tarred with that terrible monotheistic brush which gives them the sense of guilt.

They work on the supposition that human nature, like all nature is basically good. It consists in it's good-bad. It consists in the passions as much as the virtues. In Chinese there's a word *un*. I don't know how it's pronounced in Japanese. I'll write it backwards. How do pronounce that in Japanese? This means human-heartedness, humane-ness. Not in the sense of being humane in the sense of being kind necessarily, but of being human. So I say, "Oh, he's a great human being," means that's the kind of person who's not a stuffed shirt, who is able to come off it, who can talk with you on a man-to-man basis, who recognizes along with you that he is a rascal, too. And so people, men for example, when they each affectionately call a friend of theirs, "Hi, you old bastard, how you getting on?" This is a term of endearment, because they know that he shares with them what I call the "Element of Irreducible Rascality"—that we all have.

So then, if a person has this attitude, he is never going to be an over-weaning goody-goody. Confucius said, "Goody-goodies are the thieves of virtue." Because you see, if I am right, then you are wrong. And we get into a fight. What I am is a crusader against the wrong, and I'm going to obliterate you, or I'm going to demand your unconditional surrender. But if I say, "No, I'm not right, and you're not wrong but I happen to want to carry off your women. You know, you've got the most beautiful girls and I'm going to fight you for them. If I had done that, I would be very careful not to kill the girls."

In modern war we don't care. The only people who are safe are in the Air Force! They're way up there, you know, or else they've got subterranean caves they're in— women and children be gone! They can be frizzled with a Hiroshima bomb. But we sit in the plane and be safe. Now this is inhumane because we are fighting ideologically, instead of for practical things like food, and possessions, and being greedy. So that's why the Confucian would say he trusts human passions more than he trusts human virtues: righteousness, goodness, principles, and all that high-fallutin' abstractions. Let's get down to earth, let's come off it.

So then, this is why the kind of man in whom the kind of nature, the kind of human nature in which trust is put. Because you see, look, if you are like the Christians and the Jews—not so much the Jews, but mostly the Christians—who don't trust human nature, who say,

"It's fallen, it's evil, it's perverse," that puts you in a very funny position. Because if you say, "Human nature is not to be trusted," you can't even trust the fact that you don't trust it! See where you'll end out? You'll end out in a hopelessness!

Now it's true, human nature is not always trustworthy, but you must proceed on the gamble that it's trustworthy most of the time, or even 51% of the time. Because if you don't, what's your alternative? You have to have a police state. Everybody has to be watched and controlled, and then who's going to watch the police? And so, you end up this way, in China just before 250 B.C., there was a short-lived dynasty called the Ching Dynasty that lasted fifteen years. And the man decided who was the emperor of there, that he would rule everybody. Everything would be completely controlled, and his dynasty would last for a thousand years. And it was a mess. So the Hun Dynasty, which lasted from 250 B.C. to 250 A.D. came into being, and the first thing they did was to abolish all laws, except about two. Q. What were those? A. You know, elementary violence... you mustn't go around killing people and things like that, or robbing, but all the complexity of law. And this Hun Dynasty marked the height of Chinese civilization—the real period of great, great sophistication and peace... China's Golden Age. I may be over-simplifying it of course, but all historians do. But this, this was a marvelous thing you see. It's based on this whole idea of the humanism of the Far East—that although human beings are skalliwags, they are no more so than cats, and dogs, and birds and you must trust human nature. Because if you can't, you're apt to starve.

I've talked for long enough. What I suggest is, in these seminars that we have a brief intermission so we can stretch for five minutes or so, and then we finish this at 1 o'clock, but you can come back and ask questions in about 5 minutes time.

7

TRIBUTE TO CARL JUNG

I am sitting late at night, in a lonely cottage in the country, surrounded by many favorite books which I've collected over a number of years. And as I look up at the shelves I see that there's a very large space occupied by the volumes of one man—Carl Gustav Jung, who left this world not more than a few weeks ago. I'd like to talk tonight about some of the great things that I feel Jung has done for me, and also the things which I feel to be his enduring contributions toward the science of psychology, of which he was such a great master.

I began to read Jung when I first began to study Eastern philosophy in my late adolescence, and I'm eternally grateful to him for what I would call a sort of balancing influence on the development of my thought. As an adolescent, in rebellion against the sterile Christianity in which I was brought up, I was liable to go absolutely overboard for exotic and foreign ideas until I read the extraordinarily wise commentary that he wrote to Richard Wilhelm's translation of the Chinese Taoist text called, *The Secret of the Golden Flower*. It was Jung who helped me to remind myself that I was, by upbringing and by tradition, always a Westerner, and I couldn't escape from my own cultural conditioning. This inability to escape was not a kind of prison, but was the endowment of one's being with certain capacities, like one's arms and legs, and mouth, and teeth, and brain, which could always be used constructively. I feel it's for this reason that I have always remained, for myself, in the position of the comparative philosopher, wanting to balance East and West rather than to go overboard with enthusiasm for exotic imports. There are aspects of Jung's work far beyond this that I want to discuss.

First of all, I want to call attention to one fundamental principle that underlies all his work, and that was most extraordinarily exemplified in Jung, himself, as a person. This is what I would call his recognition of the polarity of life. That is to say, his resistance to what is, to my mind, the disastrous and absurd hypothesis that there is in this universe, a radical and absolute conflict between good and evil—light and darkness that can never, never, never be harmonized.

Obviously, when certain crimes and catastrophes occur, human emotions are deeply and rightly aroused. And I would, for myself say, that were I in any situation where inhuman acts were occuring, I would be roused to a degree of fury that I can hardly imagine in my present existence. But I know it would come out from me. I would oppose those sorts of atrocities with all the energy that I have, and if I was trapped in such a situation, I would fight it to the end. But at the same time, I would recognize the relativity of my own emotional involvement. I would know that I was fighting in the same way, shall we say, that a spider figts a wasp, insects which naturally prey upon one another, and fight one another. But as a human being I would not be able to regard my adversary as a metaphysical devil—that is to say, one who represented the principle of absolute and unresolvable evil.

I think this is the most important thing in Jung—that he was able to point out that to the degree that you condemn others, and find evil in others, you are, to that degree, unconscious of the same thing in yourself—or at least of the potentiality of it. There can be dictators and tyrants, just because there are people who are unconscious of their own dark sides, and they project that darkness outward to whatever enemy there may be. And they say, "There is the darkness. It is not in me, and therefore because the darkness is not in me, I am justified in annihilating this enemy whether it be with atom bombs or gas chambers, or what-not." To the degree that a person becomes conscious that the evil is as much in himself as in the other, to this same degree he is not likely to project it on to some scapegoat, and commit the criminal acts of violence upon other people.

Now this is to me the primary thing that Jung saw: that in order to admit, and *really* accept and understand the evil in oneself, one had to be able to do it without being an enemy to it. As he put it, you had to accept your own dark side. And he had this preeminently in his own character.

I had a long talk with him back in 1958, and I was enormously impressed with one who's obviously very great, but at the same time with whom everyone could be completely at ease. There are so many great people, great in knowledge, or great in what is called holiness, with whom the ordinary individual feels rather embarrassed. He feels inclined to sit on the edge of his chair, and feel immediately judged by this person's wisdom or sanctity.

Jung managed to have wisdom, and I think also sanctity, in such a way that when other people came into it's presence they didn't feel judged. They felt enhanced, encouraged, and invited to share in a common life. And there was a sort of twinkle in Jung's eye that gave me the impression that he knew himself to be just as much a villain as everybody else. There's a nice German word, *hintergedanker*, which means, a thought in the very far, far back of your mind. Jung had a hintergedanker in the back of his mind which showed in the twinkle in his eye. It showed that he knew and recognized what I sometimes call, "The Element of Irreducible Rascality" in himself. And he knew it so strongly, and so clearly, and in a way, so lovingly, that he would not condemn the same thing in others, and therefore would not be led into those thoughts, feelings, and acts of violence towards others, which are always characteristic of the people who project the devil in themselves upon the outside, upon somebody else, upon the scapegoat.

Now this made Jung a very integrated character. In other words, he was a man who was thoroughly with himself. Having seen and accepted his own nature profoundly, he had a kind of unity and absence of conflict in his own nature, which had this additional complication that I find so fascinating. He was the sort of man who could feel anxious, and afraid, and guilty, without being ashamed of feeling this way. In other words, he understood that an integrated person is not a person who simply eliminated the sense of guilt, or the sense of anxiety from his life—who is fearless, and wooden, and a kind of sage of stone. He's a person who feels all these things, but has no recrimination against himself for feeling them.

This is to my mind a profound kind of humor. As you know, in humor, there's always a certain element of malice. There was a talk given on the Pacifica stations just a little while ago, which was an interview with Al Capp, who made the point that he felt that all humor was fundamentally malicious. Now there's a very high kind of humor, which is to laugh at oneself. The real humor is not jokes at the expense of others, it's always jokes at the expense of oneself, and of course it has an element of malice in it. It has malice towards oneself: the recognition of the fact that behind the social role that you assume—

behind all your pretentions to being either a good citizen, or a fine scholar, or a great scientist, or a leading politician, or physician, or whatever you happen to be— behind this facade, there is a certain element of the unreconstructed bum. Not as something to be condemned and wailed over, but as something to be recognized as contributive to one's greatness, and to one's positive aspect, in the same way that manure is contributive to the perfume of the rose. Jung saw this, and Jung accepted this.

I want to read a passage from one of his lectures, which I think is one of the greatest things he ever wrote, and which has been a very marvelous thing for me. It was in a lecture he delivered to a group of clergy in Switzerland, a considerable number of years ago, and he writes as follows:

"People forget that even doctors have moral scruples, and that certain patients' confessions are hard, even for a doctor to swallow, yet the patient does not feel himself accepted unless the very worst in him is accepted too. No one can bring this about by mere words, it comes only through reflection, and through the doctor's attitude towards himself, and his own dark side.

If the doctor wants to guide another, or even accompany him a step of the way, he must feel with that person's psyche. He never feels it when he passes judgement. Whether he puts his judgements into words, or keeps them to himself makes not the slightest difference. To take the opposite position, and to agree with the person offhand, is also of no use, but estranges him as much as condemnation.

✗ Feeling comes only through unprejudiced objectivity. This sounds almost like a scientific precept, and it could be confused with a purely intellectual, abstract attitude of mind, but what I mean is something quite different. It is a human quality, a kind of deep respect for the facts, for the man who suffers from them, and for the riddle of such a man's life. The truly religious person has this attitude. He knows that God has brought all sorts of strange and inconceivable things to pass, and seeks in the most curious ways to enter a man's heart. He therefore senses in everything the unseen presence of the Divine Will. This is what I mean by "Unprejudiced Objectivity." It is a moral achievement on the part of the doctor, who ought not to let himself be repelled by sickness and corruption.

We cannot change anything unless we accept it. Condemnation does not liberate—it oppresses. And I am the oppressor of the person I condemn, not his friend and fellow sufferer. I do not in the least mean to say that we must never pass judgement when we desire to help and improve, but if the doctor wishes to help a human being, he must be able to accept him as he is, and he can do this in reality, only when he has already seen and accepted himself as he is. Perhaps this sounds very simple, but simple things are always the most difficult. In actual life, it requires the greatest art to be simple, and so acceptance of oneself is the essence of the moral problem, and the acid test of one's whole outlook on life.

That I feed the beggar, that I forgive an insult, that I love my enemy in the name of Christ—all these are undoubtedly great virtues. What I do unto the least of my brethren, that I do unto Christ. But what if I should discover that the least among them all, the poorest of all beggars, the most impudent of all offenders, yea, the very fiend himself, that these are within me, and that I myself stand in need of the arms of my own kindness, that I myself am the enemy who must be loved. What then? Then, as a rule, the whole truth of Christianity is reversed. There is then, no more talk of love and long-suffering. We say to the brother within us, "Rrrrr...", and condemn and rage against ourselves. We hide him from world, we deny ever having met this least among the lowly in ourselves, and had it been God himself who drew near to us in this despicable form, we should have denied him a thousand times before a single cock had crowed."

Well, you may think the metaphors rather strong, but I feel that they are not so needlessly, this is a very, very forceful passage—and a memorable one in all Jung's works. Trying to heal this insanity from which our culture in particular has suffered, of thinking that a human being can become hail, healthy, and holy by being divided against himself in inner conflict, paralleling the conception of a cosmic conflict between an absolute good and an absolute evil, which cannot be reduced to any prior and underlying unity.

In other words, our rage, and our very proper rage, against evil things which occur in this world must not over-step itself. For if we require, as a justification for our rage, a fundamental and metaphysical division between good and evil, we have an insane, and in a certain sense, schizophrenic universe, of which no sense whatsoever can be made. All conflict, Jung was saying, all opposition has its resolution in an underlying unity. You cannot understand the meaning of "to be," unless you understand the meaning of "not to be." You cannot understand the meaning of good, unless you understand the meaning of evil. Even St. Thomas Aquinas saw this. For he said that just as the silent pause which gives sweetness to the chant, so it is suffering, and so it is evil which makes possible the recognition of virtue. This is not, as Jung tries to explain, a philosophy of condoning the evil. To take the opposite position, he said, to agree with the patient off-hand is also of no use. That estranges him, the doctor, and estranges him, the patient, as much as condemnation.

Let me continue further reading from this extraordinary passage. "Healing may be called," Jung says, "a religious problem. In the sphere of social or national relations, the state of suffering may be civil war, and this state is to be cured by the Christian virtue of forgiveness and love of one's enemies. That which we recommend, with the conviction of good Christians, is applicable to external situations. We must also apply it inwardly in the treatment of neurosis. This is why modern man has heard enough about guilt and sin. He is sorely beset by his own bad conscience, and wants rather, to know how he is to reconcile himself with his own nature—how he is to love the enemy in his own heart, and call the wolf his brother. The modern man does not want to know in what way he can imitate Christ, but in what way he can live his own individual life, however meager and uninteresting it may be.

It is because every form of imitation seems to him deadening and sterile, that he rebels against the force of tradition that would hold him to well-trodden ways. All such roads, to him, lead in the wrong direction. He may not know it, but he behaves as if his own individual life were God's special will which must be fulfilled at all costs. This is the source of his egoism, which is one of the most tangible evils of the neurotic state. But the person who tells him he is too egoistic has already lost his confidence, and rightly so, for that person has driven him still further into his neurosis. If I wish to effect a cure for my patients, I am forced to acknowledge the deep significance of their egoism.

I should be blind indeed if I did not recognize it as a true will of God. I must even help the person to prevail in his egoism. If he succeeds in this, he estranges himself from other people—he drives them away, and they come to themselves, as they should—for they were seeking to rob him of his sacred egoism. This must be left to him, for it is his strongest and healthiest power. It is, as I have said, a true will of God, which sometimes drives him into complete isolation. However wretched this state may be, it also stands him in good stead for in this way alone, can he get to know himself, and learn what an invaluable treasure is the love of his fellow beings. It is, moreover, only in the state of complete abandonment and loneliness that we experience the helpful powers of our own natures." End of quote.

This is a very striking example of Jung's power to comprehend and integrate points of view, as well as psychological attitudes that seem on the surface to be completely antithetical. For example, even in his own work, when devoting himself to the study of Eastern philosophy, he had some difficulty in comprehending the, let's say, Buddhistic denial of the reality of the ego. But you can see that in practice what he was actually trying to get at, was moving towards the same position that was intended in both the Hindu and the Buddhist philosophy about the *nature* of the ego.

Just for example, as the Hindu will say that the "I" principle in man, it is not really a separate ego, but an expression of the universal life of Brahman, or the God-head. So Jung is saying here, that the development of the ego in man is a true will of God. And it is only by following the ego and developing it to its full extent, that one fulfills the function which, you might say, is a temporary illusion in man's psychic life. He goes on and says: "When one has several times seen this development at work, one can no longer deny that what was evil has turned to good, and that which seemed good has kept alive the forces of evil. The arch-demon of egoism leads us along the royal road to that in-gathering which religious experience demands. What we observe here is a fundamental law of life. And it is this that makes possible the reunion of the warring halves of the personality, and thereby brings the civil war to an end." End of quote.

In other words, he was seeing that, as Blake said, "A fool who persists in his folly will become wise." That the development of egoism in man is not something to be overcome or better integrated by opposition to it, but by following it. It's almost, isn't it, the principle of Judo— not overcoming what appears to be a hostile force by opposing it, but by swinging with the punch, or rolling with the punch. And so, by following the ego, the ego transcends itself, and in this moment of insight the great Westerner, who comes out of the whole tradition of human personality, which centers it upon the ego, upon individual separateness, by going along consistently with this principle, comes to the same position as the Easterner. That is to say, to the point of view where one sees conflict, which at first sight had seemed absolute, as resting upon a primordial unity, and thereby attaining a profound, unshakeable, peace of the heart, which can nevertheless contain conflict, not a peace that is simply static and lifeless, but a peace that passes understanding.

Jung began to see them, I think, in a primitive way. I think his archetypes are perhaps still not at the deepest level of the patterns that underly the world—and it's interesting that in the C.G. Jung commentary, that he wrote to a translation of a Chinese classic by Richard Wilhelm, called, *The Secret of the Golden Flower*. You may remember that in that commentary he takes out the very fascinating problem of the dangers inherent in the adoption of Oriental ways of life by Westerners—but more particularly, the adoption of Oriental spiritual practices such as Yoga. I remember I learned a great deal from that essay, and appreciated it very much in ever so many ways, because even in my own fascination with forms of Oriental philosophy, I've never been tempted to forget that I'm a Westerner. But, as I think this essay over, I'm not sure that Jung discouraged the practice of Yoga for quite the right reasons.

I've found so often, the difficulty in Jung's ideas lies in his theory of history, which is, I feel, a hang-over from 19th century theories of history encouraged by Darwinism. Namely that there's a sort of orderly progression from the ape, through the primitive, to the civilized man. And of course, naturally, at that time, that was all hitched in with the theory of progress. It was highly convenient for the cultures of Western Europe, which were then one up on everybody else, to consider themselves in the line of progress. When they visited the natives of Borneo and Australia, and so on, they would feel that they were perfectly justified in appropriating their lands, and dominating them, because they were giving them the benefits of the last word in evolution.

Therefore, under the influence of that sort of theory of history, which is felt in the work of both Freud and Jung, one gets the feeling of there being a kind of progressive development of human consciousness. Jung is charitable enough to assume that because the Chinese and Indian are immeasurably older than ours, they've had the possibility of far more sophistication in psychic development, even though he feels, and probably rightly, that there are things they can learn from us. But the reason why he discourages the Westerner from the practice of Yoga is, he says, "This is a discipline for a far older culture than ours, which along certain lines, has progressed much further, and has learned certain things that we haven't mastered at all yet." And as he points out, when somebody embraces Vedanta, or Theosophy, or any Yoga school in the West, and tries to master a discipline of concentration in which they have to oust from their consciousness all wandering thoughts, he says that this, for a Westerner, may be a very dangerous thing indeed—because just exactly what the Westerner may need to do, is to allow free reign to his wandering thoughts, and his imagination, and his fantasy. Because it's only in this way that he can get in touch with his unconscious, and that his unconscious will not leave him in peace until he gets in touch with it. And Jung assumes the members of Oriental cultures have done this long before they went in for Yoga practice.

Now I don't think this is quite true. But I do think there are other reasons why Western people need to exercise a good deal of discrimination and caution in adopting Eastern disciplines and ways of life. In other words, it's rather like the problem of taking medicine. You know, if you don't feel very well, and you go to a friend's medicine cabinet, and you sort of look it over, and you see bottles of medicine in there, and you say, "I'm sick, I need medicine." So you take some medicine, any medicine will do—but it won't. And according to what's the matter with you, so the medicine has to be prescribed.

I don't think that the things which some of the Eastern disciplines are designed to cure are quite the same things that we need. It's fundamental to my view of the nature of such forms of discipline as Buddhism and Taoism, that there are ways of liberation from a specific kind of confinement. That is to say, there are ways of liberation from what I've sometimes called the *social hypnosis*.

Every culture and every society as a group of people in communication with each other has certain rules of communication, and from culture to culture these rules differ in just the same way that languages differ. And a culture can hold together on very, very different kinds of rules. I won't say *any* kinds of rules, but very different kinds of rules, always provided that the members agree about them, whether they're forced to agree, whether they agree tacitly, or whatever the reason may be. These rules are, in a way, very much like the rules of a game. In other words, take a game like chess. You can have the kind of chess we play, with an eight-square board, or you can have the kind of chess that the Japanese play with a nine-square board. It doesn't make any difference, so long as you both play on the same board and by the same rules. Chess is a game, and in the same way the development of human cultures is also in a way a game—that is to say, the elaboration of a form of life and the fun of it, in a way, is the fun of elaborating it in just some interesting form, as the same is the fun of a game. The fun of a game is that it has a certain interest. But it doesn't follow that the rules of the game correspond to the actual structure of human nature, or to the laws of the universe. Because in every culture it's necessary to impress upon especially its younger members that these rules jolly well have to be kept, they are usually, in some way or other connected with the laws of the universe, and given some sort of divine sanction. There are indeed cultures in which the senior members of the group realize that that's a hoax, that that's as if it's made-up, and is done to terrify the young. When they become senior members of the culture themselves, they see through the thing, but they don't let on, they keep it quiet. They don't let out to those who are supposed to be impressed that this was really a hoax to get them to behave.

Well anyway, after a great deal of careful study I've come to the conclusion that the function of these ways of liberation is basically to make it possible for those who have the determination (and we'll see why in a while), to be free from the social hypnosis.

If you were a member of the culture of India at almost any time between maybe 900 B.C. and 1800 A.D., it would be, for you, a matter of common sense, about which everybody agreed, that you were under the control of a process called *Karma.* Not exactly a law of cause and effect, but a process of cosmic justice whereby every fortune that occurred to you would be the result of some action in the past that was good, and every misfortune that occurred to you would be the result of some action in the past that was evil. Furthermore, that this action in the past might not have been done in this present life, but in a former life. It was simply axiomatic to those people that they were involved in a long, long process of reincarnation, reaping the rewards and punishments. There was not only the possibility of being reincarnated again in the human form, but if you were exceedingly good, you might be born in one of the heavens, the paradises, and if you were exceedingly bad you might be born for an insufferable period of years, not forever, in a purgatory. The purgatories of the Hindus and Buddhists are just as ingeniously horrible as those of the Christians.

Well, of course, everybody knows, I mean anybody who seems to have any sense, that all this imagination of post-mortem courts of justice is a way of telling people, "Well, if the secular police don't catch you, the celestial police will, and therefore you had better behave!" It's an ingenious device for encouraging ethical conduct.

Now remember, for a person brought up in that climate of feeling where everybody believes this to be true, it seems a matter of sheer common sense that it's so, and it's very difficult for a person so brought up *not* to believe that is the state of affairs. Take an equivalent situation in our own culture. It's still enormously difficult for most people to believe that space may not be Newtonian space, that is to say, a three-dimensional continuum that extends indefinitely forever. The idea of a four-dimensional curve seems absolutely fantastic, and can't even be conceived by people unversed in the mathematics of modern physics. Or again as I've often pointed out, it's very difficult for us to believe that the forms of nature are not made of some stuff called matter. That's a very unnecessary idea from a strictly scientific point of view, but it's awfully difficult for us to believe it. To believe, in other words, that there isn't this underlying stuff. Not so long ago it was practically impossible for people to conceive that the planets did not revolve around the earth encased in crystalline spheres. It took a very considerable shaking of the imagination when astronomers began to point out that this need not necessarily be so.

All right, so now let's go back to the problem of somebody living in the culture of ancient India. Here it is, it's a matter of common sense, you see, that he is going to be reborn. Now, for some perhaps exceedingly intelligent person, who for one reason or another discovers that this idea is not so. After all, when you get such disciplines as Vedanta and Buddhism, they say that the ultimate goal of the discipline is a release from the rounds of rebirth, and incidentally also (which is fundamental to it), a release from the illusion that you are a separate individual confined to this body. But so far as both of these things are concerned, they also say that the person who is liberated from the round of rebirth, as well as from the illusion of being an ego, sees that when he is liberated, the process of rebirth and the whole cosmology of reincarnation and karma, as well as the individual ego, are in a way illusions. That is to say, he sees that they are *maya*.

I would like to translate maya at this moment, not so much illusion as a playful construct, a social institution. So he sees, you see, that those things are not so, they are only pretended to be so. And you see, he ceases to believe in karma and reincarnation and all that in exactly the same way that a modern agnostic no longer believes in the resurrection of the body on the Day of Judgement. I know this to be so because, although you will get very many Hindus and Buddhists who say that they believe in reincarnation and come over here and teach as part of the doctrine of Vedanta or Buddhism, the most sophisticated and the most profound (I'll say perhaps profound, rather than sophisticated) Buddhists that I have known, have said that they don't believe in it literally at all. And so I could say, those that do believe in it, believe in it simply because it's part of their culture, and they've not yet been able to be liberated from it. It seems to me very funny indeed when Western people who become interested in Vedanta or Buddhism—in forms of discipline to liberate Hindus and Chinese people from certain social institutions—Western people adopt it, and then also adopt the ideas of reincarnation and karma—from which these systems were designed to liberate them! Of course they adopt them because they feel it's consoling that one will go on living. That wasn't the point at all. Or, that it explains something—that why one suffered in this life was not because the universe was unjust, but because you committed some misdeed in the past.

And so, Westerners who take up the Oriental doctrines in that spirit, unfortunately take up the very illusions from which these documents were supposed to be ways of deliverance. Now that may be difficult to see, just because so many practicing Hindus and Buddhists say they believe in reincarnation, and this whole process of the cycles of karma and so on. They after all, are practicing it, and they should know. When I look here, there's a certain good reason why they shouldn't. Of course I'm making an exception of the Indian or Chinese who's been educated in Western style. He ceases to believe maybe in the cosmologies of his own culture, but he's not liberated in the Buddhist sense, because in receiving a Western education he's become a victim of *our* social institutions instead, and then he's just exchanged, as it were, one trouble for another. But, when you take the situation as it stands, or as it did stand in India, isolated from Western culture, obviously no society can tolerate within its own borders the existence of a way of liberation, a way of seeing through its institutions, without feeling that such a way constitutes a threat to Law and Order.

Anybody who sees through the institutions of society, and sees them for, as it were, created fictions, (in the same way as a novel or a work of art is a created fiction). Anybody who sees that, of course could be regarded by the society as a potential menace. But then you may ask, "But if Buddhism and Vedanta, and so on were indeed ways of liberation, how could Indian or Chinese society, or Burmese society have tolerated their presence?" Well, the answer lies simply in the much misunderstood esotericism of these disciplines. In other words, those who taught them, the Masters of these disciplines, made it incredibly difficult for uninitiated people to get in on the inside.

Their method of initiating them, in a way, was to put them through trap, after trap, after trap, to see if they could find their way through. Such a master would not dream of beginning by disabusing the neophyte, and saying, "Well you know, all these things you heard from your father and mother and teachers and so on were fairytales." Oh no, indeed! He would do what is called in Buddhism, exercise the use of *Upaya*. It's a Sanskrit word meaning, 'skillful devices,' or 'skillful means,' sometimes described as giving a child a yellow leaf to stop it crying for gold. After all, when you approach one of these ways of liberation from the outside, it looks like something very, very fantastic.

Here you are literally going to be released from a literally, true and physical cycle of endless incarnations in Heavens, and Hells and all kinds of states. Therefore, naturally to do that the neophyte is ready for almost anything. And what an undertaking that must be. What a wonderful, extraordinary person you've got to become. The teacher, because the fundamental problem in this whole thing is for him to get rid of the illusion, you see, that he's a separate ego. If there's no separate ego, or sort of soul, then there's nothing to be reincarnated. The teacher has all kinds of complicated ways of doing it, but all that he really says to him is: "Well now, if you will look deeply into your ego you will find out that it is a non-ego, that yourself is the Universal Self," as he might say if he were a Vedantist. Or, if he were a Buddhist he might say, "If you look for your ego, you won't find it— so look for it, and see, and really go into it." And so he gets the man meditating, and trying by his ego to get rid of his ego.

Well, that is a beautiful trap. It can last forever—until one sees through it. In other words, this is like trying to, you know, sweep the darkness out of a room with a broom. Chuang-Tse had a nice figure for it: "beating a drum in search of a fugitive." That's to say you know, when the police go out because they had a telephone call that was a burglar. They come racing to the house with the siren, full blast, and the burglar hears it and runs away. Because, of course, to try and get rid of the ego for one's advantage in some way, is an egotistic enterprise, and you can't do it. And so of course, the student gets to the point where he begins to realize that everything he does to get rid of his ego is egotistic. This is the kind of trap in which the teacher gets him—until of course, he comes to the point of seeing that his supposed division from himself into say, "I" and "me", the controller controlling part of me, and the controlled part of me, the knower and the known, and all that, is phony.

There's no way of standing aside from yourself, in other words and as it were, "changing yourself" in that way. But he discovers this finally, and at the same time he discovers, almost at the last minute you might say, the fallacy, (or rather the fantasy nature), the game-like nature of the system of cosmology which has existed to give the basic form of the social institutions of his particular culture or society.

In other words, you may put it in another way. One of the basic things which all social rules of convention conceal is what I would call the fundamental fellowship between yes and no. Say in the Chinese symbolism of the positive and the negative, the Yang and the Yin, (you know you've seen that symbol of them together like two interlocked fishes), well, the great game, the whole pretense of most societies is that these two fishes are involved in a battle. There's the up fish and the down fish, the good fish and the bad fish. And they're out for killing. And the white fish is one of these days gonna slay the black fish. But when you see into it clearly, you realize that the white fish and the black fish go together. They're twins, they're really not fighting each other—they're dancing with each other.

That you see though, is a difficult thing to realize in a set of rules in which yes and no are the basic, and formally opposed terms. When it is explicit in a set of rules that yes and no, or positive and negative are the fundamental principles. It is implicit, but not explicit, that there is this fundamental bondage, or fellowship between the two. The theory is, you see, that if people find that out, they won't play the game anymore. I mean, supposing a certain social group finds out that its' enemy group, which it's supposed to fight, is really symbiotic to it. That is to say, the enemy group fosters the survival of the group, by pruning its population. It would never do to admit that! It would never, never do to admit the advantage of the enemy, just as George Orwell pointed out in his fantasy of the future 1984, that a dictatorial government has to have an enemy, and if there isn't one, it has to invent one. By this means, by having something to fight, you see, by having something to compete against, the energy of society to go on doing its job is stirred up. What the Buddha, or Bodhisattva type of person fundamentally is, is one who's seen through that, who doesn't have to be stirred up by hatred, and fear, and competition to go on with the game of life.

LECTURES OF
ALAN WATTS

(handwritten: CALL KELLY / DESSERT)

Essential Lecture Series I
Ego
Nothingness
Time
Death
Cosmic Drama
The More It Changes
God
Meditation

Essential Lecture Series II
We As Organism
Myself: Concept or Confusion?
Limits of Language
Intellectual Yoga
She is Black
Landscape, Soundscape
Man in Nature
Work as Play

Essential Lecture Series III
Death, Birth, and the Unborn I,II
Philosophy of Nature
Man's Place in Nature
Diamond Web
Doctorine of the Void
Historical Buddhism
Yoga Cara

Philosophy
Veil of Thoughts (Parts I-IV)
Early Chinese Zen Buddhism
(Parts I-IV)

Meditation
Philosophy of Meditation
(Parts I-IV)
Sonic Meditation (Parts I-IV)

Nationally broadcast, consult local stations for schedule.
Available also on cassette tapes at thirty five dollars per series.

Alan Watts
Electronic Educational Programs
Post Office Box 938
Point Reyes Station
California - 94956